TOURING THE OLD REDWOOD HIGHWAY

DEL NORTE COUNTY

DIANE HAWK

Published by Hawk Mountaintop Publishing
P.O. Box 88
Piercy, California 95587
hawk@saber.net

Other books by the author:

IN THE EARLY DAYS
Southern Humboldt History 1853-1920
by Margarite Cook & Diane Hawk

A GLANCE BACK
Northern Mendocino County History
by Margarite Cook & Diane Hawk

TOURING THE OLD REDWOOD HIGHWAY
MENDOCINO COUNTY
by Diane Hawk

TOURING THE OLD REDWOOD HIGHWAY
HUMBOLDT COUNTY
by Diane Hawk

Front Cover -
        Patterson Postcard #875
        On the Redwood Highway
        1000 Feet Above the Sea
        (South of Crescent City)
        Late 1920s or early 1930s
        Courtesy of Joe Leger

Printed in the United States of America

ISBN-13:   978-0-9672162-5-6
ISBN-10:   0-9672162-5-7

Back Cover -
        1941 Map of Del Norte County
        U.S. 101 & U.S. 99 and Connections
        California State Automobile Assoc.
        Courtesy of Joe Leger

TABLE OF CONTENTS

MAPS

ACKNOWLEDGEMENTS

Special thanks and gold stars go to the folks who shared their postcard collections, travel directories and maps with me. First and foremost is Irl Rickabaugh who has helped with three books now. He has supported me, shared his knowledge and helped whenever I called. Jarl deBoer, Dave Parish and Mike Knips are collectors from out of the area and have graciously helped me out. Joe Leger and Arlene Hartin not only shared their collections but like nothing more than a highway question to solve.

My husband, Norman Hawk, deserves a big pat on the back for listening to me talk about the highway for the last seven years and for his help and support.

Kudos to my good friend, Evelyn Wood, who thinks there is nothing more fun than driving really slow along sections of the road, turning around without a complaint, and looking for old businesses, landmarks and mile markers. Thanks for your input.

In researching this book there were many different organizations and individuals that helped out. Many thanks to Jerry & Gisela Rohde, the Del Norte County Historical Society and its volunteers, California Dept. of Transportation, California State Automobile Association, Redwood Empire Association, *The Daily Triplicate*, *Times Standard*, Don Pass and John Theuerkauf from Smith River National Recreation Area, Colleen Rickabaugh, Jane Wilson, Phil Carnahan, Kitty Hawk, Gary Ingles and Bruce Brunell.

Last but not least, thank you to all of the wonderful people who took time to talk to me on the telephone, e-mailed me, or met with me in person.

I would appreciate any additional information or feedback you may have about auto camps, auto courts, early motels, or service stations listed, or any that I did not locate, on the Old Redwood Highway from 1920-1960. Please write or e-mail me at:

Hawk Mountaintop Publishing
P.O. Box 88, Piercy, CA 95587
or hawk@saber.net

PREFACE

I have been living in the mountains of Mendocino County, in Northern California since 1977. My home is actually up a two mile stretch of dirt road near the town of Piercy. However, the Redwood Highway (Highway 101) is my lifeline to the world. In order to go anywhere whether it's the grocery store, gas station, doctor, or a trip to the big cities of Eureka and Ukiah, I must travel on this road. The number of times I have been on it is really staggering. But in my wildest imagination I doubt if I ever thought I would write a book about it. I can honestly say, I will never be able to travel on this road again without thinking about all of the places I have written about.

While researching an earlier book, *A Glance Back,* I was fortunate to have spent a lot of time at the Held-Poage Research Library in Ukiah, California. The reason I say fortunate is because I have made a lot of good friends there. It was at the library that the idea for this book series *"Touring the Old Redwood Highway"* came about. It seems that the history of the old resorts, auto camps and gas stations that once lined the old highway were disappearing just like the businesses had. There wasn't much left in written material or in real life. However, there were still the postcards that had been taken over the years up and down the highway. If something wasn't written about these old places soon, it would be too late. Several of the people I met at the Held-Poage were postcard collectors and they offered to share their collections if I took the project on. Yes, we knew there used to be a lot of businesses up and down the highway, but we had no idea how many it would turn out to be. It has taken almost seven years for this three book series to be completed.

I don't know how many times I have driven up and down the freeway and old highway trying to locate the businesses that once existed. As the highway was realigned and improved over the years it has totally changed the landscape in many places. This has made it extremely hard to recreate where businesses once sat or which side of the road they were really on. Address markers for each business are at the exact location or as close as I could find. An example shows the highway mileage marker along the highway or a street address on today's roads. Before each address is an E or W that designates the business sat on the east or west side of the road. On Hwy. 199 along the Smith River it is designated N or S even though the road actually travels northeast. Please keep in mind that most of the old businesses are actually on private property today.

E - 13.57 Hwy. 101

Many of the advertisements for the old auto camps, auto courts, motels and gas stations were written over a 40 year period from 1920-1960. They may list how many miles a business is from the outskirts of town or from another town. This can change from ad to ad as the city limits changed as the towns expanded over the years. Plus, they can also be different from one directory to another.

Postcards and photographs were dated with a variety of methods. Some of them were already dated when I began working with them and others were dated by the era of the cars, gas pumps, signs, etc. Sometimes, a circa is used in front of the date meaning this is an approximate time frame. On the bottom left hand corner of all of the pictures is the name of the person who contributed the item. The facts and stories in this book are as true as it is possible for history to be after so many years have elapsed. I've checked and double checked as best I could, but time and memories often make it impossible to be absolutely certain of some facts.

Now having said this, I would like to invite you on a journey. Come and join me on a trip up the old Redwood Highway. I hope that you enjoy yourself!

INTRODUCTION

Our journey on the Redwood Highway in Del Norte County (Hwy. 101) starts south of the town of Klamath near the Humboldt/Del Norte county line. The road takes you into Klamath and then heads north to Crescent City. At (or near) Crescent City the Redwood Highway actually turns inland and heads northwest all the way to Grants Pass, Oregon (Hwy. 199). However, this book will only take you as far as the Oregon border. Heading north of Crescent City to Brookings, Oregon was the Roosevelt Highway (Hwy. 101). This section of highway is not part of the Redwood Highway. It is included in this book because it is an important part of Del Norte County's highway system and has an interesting history.

Traveling along today's Redwood Highway, you can still find some of the businesses that were a part of the landscape from the 1920s to the 1960s. However, most have disappeared or are faded remnants of an earlier time. You may find an old abandoned bridge across a creek, small sections of extremely narrow highway hidden in the trees or a shell of a building that was once a thriving business. They are a glimpse back to an earlier and what we like to think of as a simpler time. The road that we know today as the Redwood Highway was a long time in coming. In 1907, there were less than 300 registered automobiles in the entire state and 1,000 by 1910. That same year, the State Highway Act was signed providing for bonds to be issued for the construction and acquisition of a system of state highways.

By 1920 there was a passable road between Sausalito and Arcata. That year, automobiles had increased to 14,000 in California not counting out of state tourists who were arriving at four times this number. The last section of the Redwood Highway to be developed was the connection between Arcata and Crescent City. A great portion of this section had had no work done on it at all by the mid-1920s. Ferry service was still being used to cross the Klamath River at this time. When the Douglas Memorial Bridge across the Klamath was opened in 1926, a dream of more than 30 years was fulfilled for Del Norte residents. It was one of the last major barriers to completion of a highway in Del Norte County. The last stretches were finally completed in 1929.

In the 1920s motorists had affordable cars and there was plenty of gas. The average person could take short pleasure trips, and travel vacations with their own route, destination, timetable and roadside camping. They were anxious to hit the road and the redwoods were becoming a popular destination. Travelers took quite a bit of gear on the road with them, hauling tents, camping cots, cooking gear, spare tires, extra parts and assorted gadgets. Early vehicles were prone to flat tires, several a trip were common, and bringing spare parts was a must. Engine overheating was a common occurrence with the steep grades.

Local entrepreneurs began to advertise camping spots and it wasn't long before there was a gas pump or two, a small store or cafe and a couple of cabins. You still needed to bring your own bedding and cooking gear with you though. As travel conditions improved so did the early businesses. Cabins were upgraded and came with such amenities as hot and cold running water, heat, bathrooms, good beds and linens, garages and some even had kitchens.

During World War II business dropped dramatically along the Redwood Highway. Gas rationing was necessary and casual travel was discouraged. Once the war was over, people were ready to head out on the road again. Cars were sleeker and faster, roads were improving and travel time was being cut down. A combination of factors in the 1950s and 1960s that included travelers needs, new motels, the addition of sections of four-lane highway and damage and destruction from the 1964 flood began to change the business landscape on the old Redwood Highway. The times were changing.

Touring The Old Redwood Highway

KLAMATH

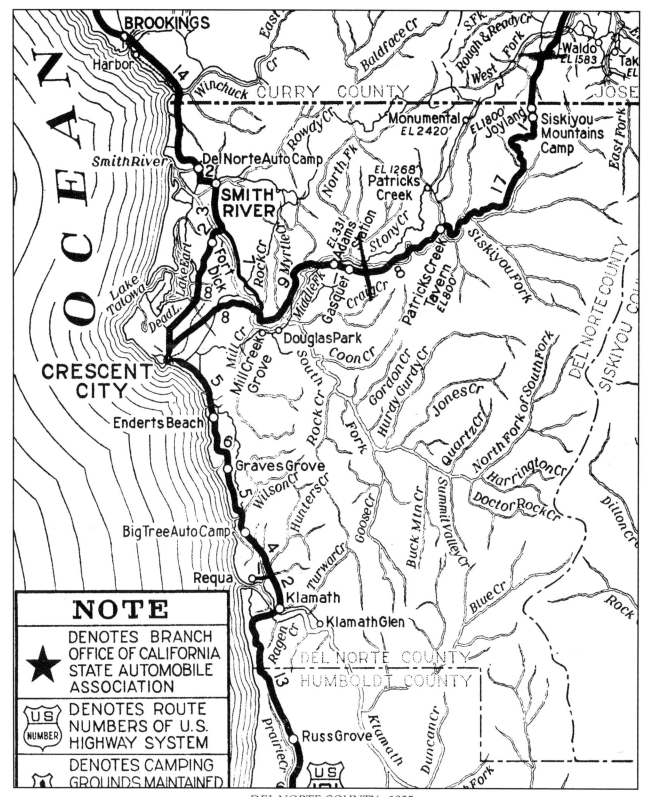

DEL NORTE COUNTY - 1935

California State Automobile Assoc. Map - U.S. 101 & U.S. 99 and Connections.
Courtesy of Joe Leger

THE CALIFORNIA REDWOOD HIGHWAY

"Some day the highway that extends from Sausalito to Crescent City will be one of the most popular of all the scenic motor drives in California. It follows the coastline almost all the way and winds in and out of the canyons of the Coast Range. Some day it will be paved for its entire length. Then it will open a country that has been growing more and more to be one of the most popular for vacations among the motorists of California.

It possesses a wealth of scenery, particularly after it reaches the canyon of the Eel River, and it passes through some of the most extensive, and some of the finest groves of redwood trees that the State can boast. Its principal drawback lies, not merely in the lack of adequate road improvements, but in the lack of accommodations for long distances in the mountains of Humboldt and northern Mendocino County.

A bridge over the Klamath is one of the keys to a great wealth of travel from Oregon and the Northwest. Now the inadequate ferry facilities, relying on tide and weather conditions, make the coast trip to Oregon one of probabilities rather than certainties.

The combination of forest and stream and sea is a wonderful sight, and the completion— the paved completion—of this California Redwood Highway will bring one of the days of congratulation to the State."

Motor Land – May 1922

STATE MAINTENANCE ON REDWOOD ROUTE BENEFITS TRAFFIC

"By August 1st maintenance crews of Division 1 expect to have finished the improvement of nearly 30 miles of unconstructed highway on Route 1 (later Hwy. 101) in northern Humboldt and southern Del Norte counties. The work which has been under way for over two months, consists of widening the existing county road at curves and the construction of additional turnouts.

The old road, inadequate for the rapidly increasing traffic of the redwood country, has been extensively improved under the new policy of State maintenance, which was authorized by the last legislature. On the section mentioned more than 100 blind curves, formerly too narrow for machines to pass, have been widened to 20 to 30 feet. Additional turnouts to the number of more than 100 have been built so that for a considerable portion of the distance a two-way road has been provided."

California Highways – July 1926
Courtesy of California Department of Transportation Library

THE REDWOOD HIGHWAY – BUILDING THE ROAD

"One of the factors affecting road construction during World War I was the stiff control exercised by the War Industries Board, which made it very difficult to ship highway materials. Furthermore, labor was scarce, since wages were high in the industries constructing ships and other war materials. During 1917 contract costs rose from 40 to 60 percent. As a result, in 1918 about 80 percent of the projects were deferred. However, California did much better than east of the Rockies, where road building was stopped almost completely. California had one advantage in its Convict Act of 1915. This law allowed the State to use certain trusted convicts on road building jobs. During the war these men were used quite effectively on several roads, including the Redwood Highway.

By 1918 paving was completed from Sausalito to Healdsburg and about 10 miles of highway in the vicinity of Ukiah. Despite the war and the terrain, most of the route north to Dyerville was either graded or under contract. There was a 10-mile section finished from Eureka to Arcata, but from Arcata north to Crescent City the route was still only in a proposed state. Beyond Crescent City there was nothing even proposed!

By 1920 there was a passable road between Sausalito and Eureka, but as late as 1925 there were still long stretchs which were unpaved. In 1923 the road between Crescent City and Grants Pass was designated US Highway Route 199 and included in the Forest Highway System. The Bureau of Public Roads made considerable improvement on the old Gasquet route between 1924 and 1926. In 1926 the State improved and realigned a sizeable piece and took over maintenance of the entire route to the Oregon line.

The State had just opened the first part of this route when the Smith River rose to the highest level ever recorded. Many sections of road were completely washed out. Fills built at great labor were swept away. Even at prices prevalent in those days repairs cost several hundred thousand dollars.

A great portion of the section between Arcata and Crescent City had no work done on it at all by the mid-1920s. In 1924 a survey was made of highway bridges needed in the State. These were indicated on a map with a little black circle where each bridge was needed. It made this section look like a bunch of grapes, with barely room for all the circles. Crossings at these points were still being made as at the Klamath River by primitive ferry, or fording.

From the mid-1920s, the story of the Redwood Highway was the careful husbanding of funds to complete the unpaved sections, and the grading and paving of those sections on which no work had yet been done. By 1930 the entire highway had been 'improved.' Unfortunately, these 'improvements' were to standards based on surveys made prior to World War I!"

California Highways & Public Works, July-Aug. 1964
Courtesy of California Department of Transportation Library

THE OLD REDWOOD HIGHWAY TO KLAMATH

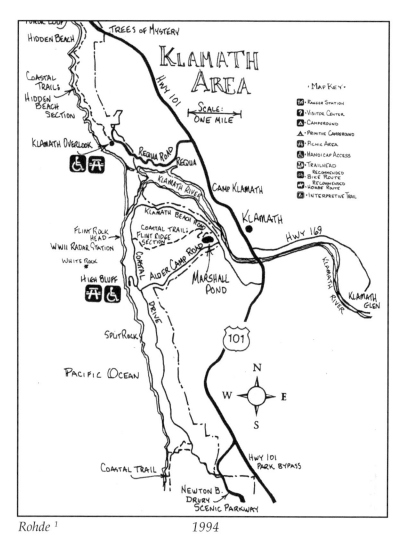

Rohde [1]   1994

Our journey starts just south of the Humboldt/ Del Norte County line. Heading north on Highway 101, take the **Newton B. Drury Scenic Parkway** (exit 753) through Prairie Creek Redwoods State Park.* This was the old Redwood Highway in Humboldt County until the bypass was completed in 1992. Make a left turn on **Coastal Drive** at about 8 miles. This partly paved road is a remnant of the Redwood Highway. Some of this road follows and crosses the old county wagon road built in the 1890s. At about 3 miles the road divides.

REQUA FERRY - The road to the left, "Coastal Drive then descends to the Klamath River Overlook at mile 6.2. A dirt road, left, leads to the remnants of **Dad's Camp**, a fishing resort that in recent years has been almost entirely washed away by the changing course of the river. Charlie and Annie Williams opened the resort in 1914; they also maintained a stop for travelers who were waiting for the **Requa Ferry**, which crossed the Klamath near here.

Coastal Drive ends at mile 6.2 of the route, opposite the entrance to Dad's Camp. **Klamath Beach Road**, paved and two-lane continues the trip; it immediately descends to the flats near the river and proceeds upstream, running by several fishing and camping resorts along the way."[2] This two mile section of Klamath Beach Road was not part of the highway but it will take you back to Alder Camp Road and the old Douglas Memorial Bridge (below).

DOUGLAS MEMORIAL BRIDGE – TOWN OF KLAMATH - Going back to **Ocean View Drive** where the road divided, the road to the right **Alder Camp Road** (not Alder Fork Road) was the Redwood Highway from 1926-1965. Follow this road to the end and you will come to a parking area and "opposite the junction is the southern end of the **Douglas Memorial Bridge**, all that remains from the 1964 flood. When the bridge opened in 1926, it closed the last gap in the coastal highway. Some 50 feet of its southern section, along with its pair of eight-ton 'California bears' (statues) remain where the highway once met the river."3 When the new bridge was built upstream in 1964-65, the highway was realigned and eliminated this coastal route.

Continue on the road for a little more than a mile and you will meet **Hwy. 101** just south of the current Klamath River Bridge.

---

* For a shorter route take Newton B. Drury Scenic Parkway exit 765 (137.00). At about a mile make a right turn on Coastal Drive. The Humboldt/Del Norte county line runs through this area.

1-3 Redwood National & State Parks – Tales, Trails, & Auto Tours, Jerry & Gisela Rohde, 1994.

DAD'S CAMP

Dad's Camp At Mouth Of Klamath River- Good Steelhead And Salmon Fishing- See "Harry" For Your Tackle

The Only Camp At The Mouth Of The Klamath - One Mile Of Ocean Front- One Quarter Mile Of River-Front

The Salmon Signs They Lead You To Dad's Place _

Irl Rickabaugh   DAD'S CAMP   *Late 1920s*

Dad's Camp was no longer on the highway once the Douglas Memorial Bridge was built (1926) and the road was changed.

Sign next to three men: UP THE BEACH TO DADS
Sign on building: EATS   TACKLE
                Homemade Pie   HOT LUNCH

Irl Rickabaugh   REQUA FERRY   *Postmark 1925*

"A day labor convict camp is located on the Klamath River above Requa and is engaged in building a new highway, of high standards of alignment and width, to connect the present county road with the proposed 'Dr. Douglas Memorial Bridge' which will be erected across the Klamath River near Requa. 150 convicts are at work at this point."

California Highways - Jan. 1924
Courtesy of California
Department of Transportation Library

History of the Requa Ferry is on page 28.

Klamath Beach Rd.
& Alder Camp Rd.

A New Redwood Highway Link

"The centuries-old calm of the virgin redwood forest along the Redwood Highway was disturbed last month by the coming of 6,000 (*actually 4,000*) people from all over the western states to witness the dedication of the newest link of the Redwood Highway—the Douglas Memorial Bridge.

This mammoth structure heralds the approach of modern development into a territory that has been heretofore somewhat isolated and inaccessible. The exact date of the opening of the bridge to travel is somewhat indefinite and will depend upon the completion of construction on three miles of highway approaching the bridge.

When the structure is opened to traffic, the matchless scenic treasures of the Redwood Empire will be available to the tourist, vacationist and traveler every month in the year. It will no longer be necessary to depend upon the uncertainties of the antiquated ferry which motor travel must use at the present time to cross the Klamath River.

The Klamath River bridge is the largest structure of its kind on the state highway system of California, and probably the largest reinforced concrete arch bridge in the world built with the piers resting on timber pile foundations. It is nearly 1,200 feet long, its central feature being five massive arches, each 210 feet in length. It has a clear roadway width of 21 feet, the roadway being 51 feet above the water of the river. The great concrete piers extend 30 feet below the low water mark where they are founded on 946 piles, driven many feet into the bed of the stream."

Motor Land – June 1926

DOUGLAS MEMORIAL BRIDGE OVER THE KLAMATH RIVER

Jarl deBoer

The Klamath Get Its Bridge

Jerry & Gisela Rohde

"The dedication of the Douglas Memorial Bridge was a spectacular event. Some 4,000 celebrants, including the club-wielding Oregon Cavemen 'in their striking picturesque costumes,' and governors Friend W. Richardson of California and Walter M. Pierce of Oregon, attended. Contestants from Hoopa and Requa competed in an Indian stick game. A special highlight was 'an exhibit of all the wild flowers in Del Norte County (that) was staged upon the bridge, and was beautiful.'

There was ample reason to rejoice for the Redwood Highway's greatest obstacle to through traffic had just been eliminated. For 50 years the only way to cross the Klamath River had been by ferry, a haphazard arrangement that at various times consisted of either a raft, a Yurok canoe, or nothing at all. Over the years the coastal trail that reached the river had grown first to a wagon road and than at last to a highway, but all traffic had come to a halt at the Klamath. Now there was a two-lane, 1,200-foot long concrete bridge to span the river, the longest such structure in the state, so that tourists, truckers, and other travelers could ride for over 400 miles, from Sausalito to Crescent City, without interruption.

There was lots of traffic waiting to make the run. The previous October some 1,000 cars a day started south from Grants Pass on their way to redwood country, although their occupants had to endure some 70 miles of merely 'magnificent' mountain roadway before they saw the first of the tall trees. From the other direction the statistics were even more impressive—more than 50,000* scenery seekers would leave Sausalito on a single Sunday or holiday, heading north on the highway for San Rafael or Santa Rosa, Ukiah or Eureka, or some other dazzling destination. The auto had come into its own, and a host of delighted drivers now had a roadway worthy of their magical machines.

Turning a rutted wagon road into the Redwood Highway hadn't been easy. Although the improvement was authorized by a bond act in 1909, work at first proceeded slowly. The railroad

Bridge dedicated on May 17, 1926.

Jarl deBoer   NORTH END DOUGLAS MEMORIAL BRIDGE   Early 1930s
Entering Town of Klamath

* I question the fact that there were 50,000 vehicles. It seems much too high a number for the 1920s.

*DOUGLAS
MEMORIAL
BRIDGE*

R 52.   THE G. H. DOUGLAS MEMORIAL BRIDGE ACROSS KLAMATH RIVER.   63081

Jarl deBoer

moved quicker, claiming the prime route through much of Humboldt and Mendocino counties, the canyon of the Middle Eel. The highway was left to run along the river's more rugged tributary, the South Fork, compelling the hard-pressed construction crews to sometimes pack in materials and equipment on muleback. Even where there was no competing rail route, the harried highway engineers often had trouble locating a convenient course; south of Crescent City, for example, the roadbed had to be carved from the crumbling coastal cliffs, while stretches through the redwoods required removing 200-ton trees and maneuvering through morasses of mud.

World War I interrupted work on the roadway, but the subsequent use of convict labor speeded construction. While construction continued on the Crescent City to Grants Pass portion of the highway, the coastal section neared completion. Only one spot was in question: the crossing of the Klamath River.

*DOUGLAS
MEMORIAL
BRIDGE'S
GOLDEN
BEARS*

Jarl deBoer

It fell to Gustave H. Douglas to do something about it. Known for many years as a dedicated doctor, he'd gained fame for having once pumped a railroad handcar 18 miles to a remote cabin, where he then saved a little girl's life. Now he took on a new challenge; after winning election to the state assembly, he made his sole cause the construction of the bridge. The effort killed him. Douglas died in office from overwork, but he'd done his job well—after his death the legislature approved his bridge bill unanimously.

Now the doctor's dream had become reality. At the dedication, his widow christened the structure and his son Donald unveiled a memorial tablet; the ceremony concluded, cars and trucks at last crossed the Klamath unaided.

For nearly 40 years traffic rolled across the great bridge. The flood of 1955 battered it. *(Flood waters completely wiped out the bridge approach on the north end.)* Then came the 1964 deluge; this time the raging water proved too much. Most of the bridge washed away."[4]

CHRISTMAS FLOODS 1964 – The Redwood Highway

"North of Eureka, in southern Del Norte County, the Klamath, always a strong, deep stream, rose rapidly and swept away the entire business section and many private homes in the town of Klamath and nearby communities. The beautiful old concrete arch bridge here, famous for its statues of California Bears on either end, was a casualty. An eyewitness of the bridge's death told Sam Helwer, district engineer, that before the structure failed, debris was backed upstream several hundred feet, although the river level was still several feet from the top of the arches. At times, small logs would come hurtling downstream, hit the floating debris, and shoot into the air completely over the structure. The pressure of the river against the debris finally pushed 400 feet of the bridge out of the way, and the debris shot downstream with a roar.

By January 8 the Army Engineers had assembled a ferry on the north bank of the river just below the devastated town of Klamath. Although hardly more than 100 vehicles were ferried daily during the first weeks, proficiency gradually increased. On Feb. 18 another 30 feet was added to the ferry, and the load limit was raised to the legal highway maximum. By this time the daily lift was more than 500 vehicles.

Photo: Looking south along U.S. 101, the Redwood Highway, with the town of Klamath in the foreground and washed-out bridge in background.

California Highways & Public Works -
Xmas Floods 1964, Jan.-Feb. 1965
Courtesy of California Department of Transportation Library

[4] *Redwood National & State Parks - Tales, Trails, & Auto Tours, Jerry & Gisela Rohde, 1994.*

Sixth Army pontoon ferry crossing Klamath River; ruined bridge upper left. Note the debris on bridge. Piers in background are for new highway bridge under construction.

From its first trip the little ferry caught the imagination of the press, and it got wide publicity over the state. This was well deserved, for it faithfully served traffic during daylight hours for more than two months, with only a few interruptions from river level changes. When the pile structure filling the broken gap on the Klamath Bridge was opened March 14, the ferry was retired after an estimated 5,527 trips across the turbulent stream. During its slightly more than two months of operation, it had carried nearly 30,000 vehicles." [5]

The new bridge across the Klamath River was built about a mile upstream and dedicated on Nov. 28, 1965. When the bridge opened for traffic it was accessed from a new section of highway that was built between the north end of Prairie Creek Redwoods State Park and Klamath. Now when you came into the Town of Klamath over the new bridge, it was on a totally different alignment than the previous road. This new section of highway eliminated the old winding coastal road.

Klamath River Bridge with temporary repairs, opened to traffic on March 14, 1965.

[5] and photos: *California Highways & Public Works, Christmas Floods 1964, Jan.-Feb. 1965.*
  Courtesy of California Department of Transportation Library.

*Keep in mind that when you cross the Klamath Bridge today on Hwy. 101, the town was not along this route. Prior to the 1964 flood, you crossed the old Douglas Memorial Bridge further downstream which brought you into town in a totally different direction. The old road ran almost perpendicular to Hwy. 101 today. In the photo below, today's highway would have run along the bottom of the mountain. To access the area where downtown Klamath once stood, make a right turn on **Hwy. 169** (**Terwer Valley**) after you cross the Klamath Bridge. Then make a left turn under the bridge and you will come across a sign for old Klamath Township. A short distance down the road is **Alder Camp Road.** This was once the Redwood Highway and the main street you see in the photos.*

TOWN OF KLAMATH

"Klamath City was established in 1851 by settlers who envisioned it as a seaport for supplying the inland mines. The bar at the river mouth proved too treacherous for large ships to cross, and within a year the town was abandoned and its 30-odd buildings—including an iron 'fort'—removed. By then, some 29 of the town's residents had died, the victims either of drowning or disagreements with the local Yuroks; Klamath City, it was said, 'lasted quick.' Next came the Klamath Indian Reservation in 1855, reinforced by Fort Ter-Wah two years later. The fort was established by then-Lieutenant George Crook, who later gained fame for his pursuit of Geronimo. Many Indians had already left the reservation before the winter of 1861-2, when a great flood washed away most of the arable land and left the nearby fort in shambles; a few months later both sites were abandoned. Squatters subsequently took over portions of the property, but they were evicted by the government in 1877 during a bitter dispute.

Activity then shifted downstream to Requa, where the recently established ferry crossed the river. After a lapse of nearly 50 years, Klamath again came to life in 1926, when the brand-new Douglas Memorial Bridge brought the Redwood Highway past the old townsite; soon a sizable string of stores lined the roadsides.

The 1955 flood removed 'entire rows' of buildings from the town, but the resilient residents rebuilt. A bigger flood hit in 1964, and this time only one shop was left standing; when federal disaster relief was slow in coming, many of the town's inhabitants left. The washed-out bridge was replaced upstream by a new structure and the town relocated on higher ground east of the rerouted highway." [6]

Left Side:
D.N. Brack -
Richfield Service
Klamath Bakery

Right Side in order:
Ed Fiesters Place
Klamath Garage
Bridge Cafe
Store - Groceries

Irl Rickabaugh   TOWN OF KLAMATH   *Late 1920s*

[6] *Redwood National & State Parks, Tales, Trails, & Auto Tours, Jerry & Gisela Rohde, 1994.*

CATES BROTHERS RIVERSIDE AUTO CAMP – STOP & FISH TRAILER & TENT CAMP

Irl Rickabaugh

1930

About 1938 – Cates Brothers
At north end of Klamath Bridge, 64 miles north of Eureka. Accommodations for campers and house trailers. 50 cents per night per car or trailer. Showers, electricity, lavatories, wood, laundry, outboard motor boats.

Irl Rickabaugh

Late 1920s

CATES BROS.
River Side Auto Park
Klamath   California
Ferry Schedule to Fishing Grounds:
Leave: 6 8,10, A.M. – 12:20, 2,4, 6, P.M.
Return: 7,9,11, A.M. – 1, 3, 5, 7, P.M.
     Rates: Round Trip – 25¢
     Those hiring boats – Free
Restaurant and Lobby at Each Place
     . Free Parking at Dock!

Irl Rickabaugh

The Humboldt Times – July 2, 1939

Jarl deBoer   *FISHING THE MOUTH OF THE KLAMATH*

DEL NORTE COUNTY STREAMS ALIVE WITH FISH

"As this is not a tourist town and the district makes no attempt to attract the traveler, few have had the pleasure of a real day's fishing here.

South of Crescent City is the Klamath River, 23 miles, and the village of Requa. The salmon run is now on and many tons of fish are being caught each day. These salmon are the famous Chinook, noted for their gameness and flavor.

Two enterprising citizens of Requa have started what they call a 'tourist cannery.' They do not can tourists, but do can the fish they catch. If you should, and nearly everyone who tries does, catch a few twenty-pounders, you take your catch to the cannery and in an hour's time you have a few cases to take home to substantiate your fish story.

If you want trout or steelhead, go to Smith River, and by the way, it is only three miles to the ocean from the town and yet it never gets cold there, or if you want salmon go to Requa, on the Klamath.

You can stop at Giant Redwood Park if you wish (six miles north of Requa), and be out of the cold. Drive back and forth each day and do your fishing, or you will find an excellent hotel at Requa, also an auto camp on the south bank where boats may be rented."

Redwood Highway Review – Sept. 24, 1926

Jarl deBoer

PIWASON LODGE – KLAMATH HOTEL

I don't know exactly when the Piwason Lodge was built but it shows up in a 1929 photograph of the town of Klamath. It was located on the northeast side of the Douglas Memorial Bridge and set back a little ways from the highway. In the late 1940s, the owner of the Klamath Hotel built the Klamath Hotel Court. The court was located right on the highway and the hotel was behind it.

Irl Rickabaugh   *1930s*

KLAMATH HOTEL COURT – RIVERSIDE COURT

Mike Knips   *1950s*

MAXEY'S MOTEL

Irl Rickabaugh   *MAXEY'S MOTEL*   *Late 1940s*

1954 – *Redwood Empire Assoc.*
MAXEY'S MOTEL—In the heart of Klamath.
Modern accommodations with kitchens and
showers. C.O. Maxey, owner.

Crescent City H.S. Yearbook - 1952

JOHNSON'S AUTO CAMP

Irl Rickabaugh   ENTRANCE TO JOHNSON'S AUTO CAMP   *Late 1930s*

Early 1930s – *Redwood Empire Assoc.*
Johnson's Auto Camp
Center of town. Cabins with showers and toilets, electric lights, water, stoves, fuel. Close to famous Klamath River fishing. Hunting, swimming, boating. Stores and restaurants nearby. Rates. $1.50 for 2; $2.00 for 4.

Joe Leger   KLAMATH   *Mid-1940s*
Johnson's was located on the right just past the Texaco sign.

MYERS MOTEL

The earliest information found for the Myers Motel was 1953.

Joe Leger   MYERS MOTEL   1950s

Irl Rickabaugh   NORTH END OF KLAMATH LOOKING SOUTH   Circa 1940
Mortensen's first gas station on left (see page 19).

KLAMATH SERVICE STATION & MODERN CABINS – MORTENSEN'S CABINS

Irl Rickabaugh   MORTENSEN'S   Early 1940s

1934 – *Shell Directory*
Klamath Service
Private toilets and showers, kitchen with dishes, restaurant and grocery near. Open garages. $1.50-$4.75.

About 1938 - Mortensen's Cabins Klamath 64 miles north of Eureka. 7 housekeeping cabins, with bedroom, kitchenette, shower, toilet. Rates $2.00 and up. Linen 50 cents. Dishes 25 cents.

BERG'S CAMP

1952 – *Redwood Empire Assoc.*
Berg's Camp
Oldest spot in Klamath. Klamath's favorite fishing center. Cabins with kitchen facilities or hotel rooms. Cool and shady. Boats and Evinrude motors. Phone Klamath 361. H.W. Berg.

THE FLOOD OF 1955

"Rains which pounded the area relentlessly during the third week of December sent the Klamath surging upward. The low ground at the mouth of the river was flooded, and more than 1,000 persons driven from their homes. Traffic over U.S. 101 south to Eureka was stopped by the high water, as the south approach to the Douglas Bridge was washed away and earth slides loosened by the rain blocked the Redwood Highway. Damage ran into the millions of dollars in Del Norte County.

The communities of Klamath, Klamath Glen and Orick were evacuated and suffered fearful damage. Klamath was inundated. On the morning of the 22nd, only the second stories and roofs protruded above the churning, muddy water. A reporter from the *Triplicate*, who flew over the area, observed that it was 'a horrible, sickening sight, as the highest flood water in the history of the great Klamath River smashed and swept all before its wild, muddy flow. Debris was in sight everywhere. Logs, trees, sides of houses, propane tanks, in fact almost everything, was observed being carried down the river.'

The rains providentially ceased on the 21st, and the Klamath crested the next afternoon. President Dwight D. Eisenhower on Christmas Eve proclaimed the flood-ravaged region in the Pacific Northwest a major disaster area."

"History Basic Data, Redwood National Park," prepared by Edwin C. Bearss, Sept. 1, 1969.

Irl Rickabaugh   TOWN OF KLAMATH

Photo is looking south along the Redwood Highway in downtown Klamath. The bridge is just out of sight on the top. On the upper right was the old Cates Brothers building and across the street was the Klamath Hotel and Riverside Court. On the left side there are some buildings that are totally submerged.

GLOVER'S AUTO CAMP

1926 – *Redwood Empire Assoc.*
Glover's Camp – Gloverdale
Open all year. Capacity 75.
Cabins furnished & unfurnished.
Bill & Jess Glover.

About 1938
Glover's Auto Camp
1/2 mile from Klamath Bridge,
64 ½ miles north of Eureka. 12
cabins with electric lights,
stoves, ovens, fuel, showers,
toilets, spring water. Rates $1.50
and up. Swimming, fishing and
hunting.

Redwood Empire Assoc. - 1926   DEL NORTE COUNTY

See ALL *the* REDWOOD EMPIRE

"THE REDWOOD EMPIRE is 'America's Newest National Playground,' having been made accessible only in recent years. You should plan to see the entire Pacific Coast, but be sure to include the Redwood Empire—the newest of a number of major attractions and national parks scattered throughout the Pacific Coast states of California, Oregon and Washington, and the Canadian Province of British Columbia (via San Francisco).

The most kaleidoscopic succession of wondrously enchanting vistas ever concentrated in one single tour area will thrill the sightseer and lover of nature in the Redwood Empire.

The fisherman and the huntsman will find keen, exhilarating sport in the Redwood Empire. In this vast 'Sportsmen's Paradise' there is close to 2,000 miles of trout streams, and many miles of lake, ocean and surf fishing.

Numerous golf courses, with natural hazards, green carpeted fairways and sporty features are scattered throughout the Redwood Empire.

Other popular sports include horseback riding, hiking, swimming, boating, canoeing, camping, mountaineering, hunting, fishing and all other vacation sports.

97% of the world's redwoods are found in the Redwood Empire. These giant trees are thousands of years old and reach a maximum height of 364 feet and diameter of 30 feet.

These monarchs of the ages are the oldest living things on the face of the earth. The Redwood Highway itself is lined with over 100 miles of redwood giants.

To travel the Redwood Empire, an automobile is not necessarily required. Modern, regular, reliable and reasonably priced motor stage, railroad and rent-car facilities are available.

The Redwood Empire offers the climatically pleasant and scenic major routings between California, Oregon, Washington and British Columbia (via San Francisco)."

Redwood Empire Association – 1931

LARSON'S CABINS – COLO-HIO COURT

1934 – *Shell Directory*
Larson's Cabins
3/4 mile north (Klamath). Private toilets and showers, kitchen with dishes, grocery near. Open garages. $1.50-$2.50. Extra charge for bedding and linen.

1949 – *Redwood Empire Assoc.*
Colo-Hio Court
On the Klamath three-quarters of a mile north of Klamath on 101 Highway. Boats and motors for rent. Guides at your disposal. Cabins with housekeeping facilities. Cafe and service station in conjunction. Open year' round. Richard and Miriam Uhl.

Irl Rickabaugh   LARSON'S   1940
Sign over gas pumps: *Coffee Shop -- Groceries -- Fishing Tackle*
The woman on the billboard is advertising: New! Free! Scenic Views.

CAMP KLAMATH

North of 6.0 Hwy. 101

Camp Klamath opened around 1935 and was wiped out in the 1964 flood. It was demolished and reopened as a trailer park only. While traveling on the Redwood Highway in 2004, I saw the last remaining Camp Klamath sign removed. It was the only shred of evidence that there had ever been a business there.

1935 – *Shell Directory*
Camp Klamath
1 mile north Klamath. Private toilets and showers, kitchen with dishes, restaurant and grocery near. Open garages. $1.50-$3.50. Extra charge for bedding and linen.

1940s – *National Auto Club*
Camp Klamath
17 frame cottages, 14 with toilet, 7 with shower, all with kitchens. $2.00-$2.50 including bedding. Open April to December. No camping space.

SAFFORD ISLAND AUTO CAMP

Joe Leger   SAFFORD ISLAND   Mid-1930s

> **Safford Island Auto Camp** Tony Troyak, Prop. – One mile north of Klamath. Two entrances—follow the sign of the big fish. Best equipped and most comfortable camp on the river. Big trees. A sheltered camp on level grassy soil. Excellent fleet of boats for hire. Store and tent grounds. Green the year-around.

The Humboldt Times - Sept. 14, 1933

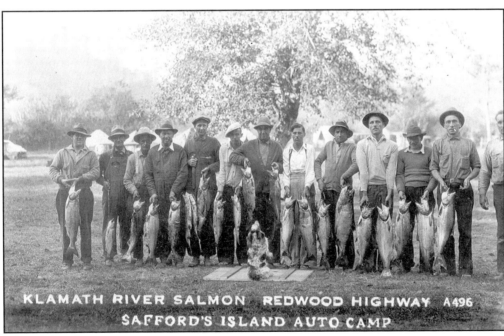

Irl Rickabaugh

Safford Island was 83 acres of some of the finest land on the Klamath River. At one time, several families lived here and had gardens. Other parts of the island were used as a campground, cow pasture and a baseball diamond. The Fisherman's Cannery also operated here for three seasons. Almost half of the island was washed away in the 1955 flood and the remaining land disappeared in the 1964 flood.

SPORTSMAN'S PARADISE TRAILER & AUTO CAMP

1935 – *Conoco Travel Bureau*
Sportsman's Paradise
2 cottages, $1.00.

About 1938 – Sportsman's Paradise
2 miles north of Klamath. Electrical
connections, shower, toilets, camping space,
50 cents per night for trailer or car.

Mike Knips
SPORTSMAN'S PARADISE AUTO CAMP
On the banks of the Klamath - Frank Bosch, Prop.
About 1930

WHERE TO GET ROAD INFORMATION

"It is foolish to write a log of a highway that is under rapid and intensive construction. A bad place today is fixed tomorrow. A new place is broken and another report is out as to the condition of the road, for the next day's traveling. The timid driver will dash around a blind curve on the wrong side of the road, and have a minor collision which he pictures as an almost fatal accident, and to everyone he meets he paints his 'narrow escape.'

If anyone desires to get honest information sufficient to guide him over any highway, all he need do is go to the stage offices and ask what kind of stages they are putting over the road, what time they are making and if they are going through without change and on their own power.

If big, 16-passenger *(auto)* stages can make schedule time over the worst part of the Redwood Highway, anybody with any kind of a car can get through safely, and see the most gorgeous scenery to be found on any highway in America.

There is the person who is scared to death of curves. He will admit he is out to see the scenery, but he forgets or doesn't realize that nature never put any scenery on straight roads. If there is any scenery on straight roads, man put it there."

Redwood Highway Review - 1928

INDIAN MARATHON TOUTED REDWOOD HIGHWAY

"Run when you can, walk when you wish and sleep if you have to. Finish in 15 days. Don't accept lifts and don't get off the Redwood Highway. Those were the rules of the race. The year was 1927. The prize was $1,000. The 11 runners were all Indians—some Zuni from New Mexico, the others representing towns along the route. The distance was 480 miles.

In the 1920s, when the world of California's North Coast was still comparatively young and innocent, people could get very excited about an event such as this. They crowded the roadsides in the towns along the highway, cheering for hometown heroes who were running what still seems amazing distances for what now seems very little money, but a lot of tribal bragging rights. The Indian Marathon was the first 'hurrah' for the Redwood Empire Association (REA), organized to promote the new Redwood Highway, a road that had been bulldozed, pieced and patched together over a dozen years to open a coastal route for a new breed of traveler, one that drove an automobile.

The race was conceived to bring nationwide attention to this newly named 'Redwood Empire.' Credit for the idea went to REA member Harry Lutgens, publisher of the San Rafael Independent, credit for some of the financial backing to Charles Howard of Willits' Ridgewood Ranch and Seabiscuit fame, but credit for the promotion, which was successful beyond hope, went to a former Santa Rosan named C.C. 'Charlie' Pyle.

The runners from the Zuni nation were famous for their ability to cover long desert distances. The plan was to test the mettle of the California runners against them. Much attention focused on an aging Zuni named Melika, who was 55 years old. Melika gained national attention by running the 950 miles from Gallup to San Francisco—to 'warm up' for the coastal run."[7]

"At 10:00 a.m. on June 14, (1927) all was in readiness at (San Francisco) City Hall. The eight Indians from Happy Camp became known by their Indian names. They were Rushing Water, Flying Cloud, Fighting Stag, Falcon, Mad Bull, Thunder Cloud, Sweke Eagle and Big White Deer. (They were running for the Oregon Cavemen.) The three Zunis from New Mexico were Jamon running for Marvelous Marvin; Melika for Willits and Chochee for Humboldt. A revolver was discharged signifying the beginning of the historic marathon. There was much fanfare as the Indians ran to the ferryboat dock to embark on their only ride for several days.

Flying Cloud, one of the Karoks, was leading the next day, June 15, with the three Zunis behind and the other Karoks trailing. By Thursday, June 16, Mad Bull, a Karok, had taken the lead. He was four miles south of Willits, 138 miles from San Francisco. Flying Cloud was eight miles behind and Rushing Water was in third place. The Zunis were falling behind. Jamon, the youngest of the Zunis, had severe foot blisters. He was forced to give up, fearing permanent injury. The two older Zunis, Melika and Chochee were running together in fourth place. On June 17, a dispatch from Laytonville reported Mad Bull had gone 37 miles during the night and was 191 miles north of San Francisco. He was leading Melika and Chochee by 12 miles. Rushing Water and Falcon had been picked up by the course physician for medical attention, then returned to their stopping places to resume the marathon.

When Mad Bull reached Pepperwood, he was only five miles ahead of the 48-year-old Chochee who represented Humboldt County. Melika was third at this time. Flying Cloud was next at a point six miles south of Dyerville but was suffering from a bad knee. Most of the Indians complained of the discomfort of inhaling carbon monoxide gas emitted from the exhaust of passing vehicles on this narrow road. Nevertheless all were applauded along the way by enthusiastic bystanders.

The residents of Fortuna were excited at having the Indian runners coming through their town.

They were to be alerted by the city's fire siren when the first runner reached the city limits. The businessmen had made a donation of $100 to be presented to the first runner through Fortuna that went on to finish the race.

An hour before Mad Bull reached the Eureka Inn on Saturday, June 18, the sirens began blowing. When the runner arrived he was greeted enthusiastically by 3,000 persons and received a kiss from Miss Redwood Empire (Little Fawn).

From Orick to Requa they were forced into an obstacle race due to highway construction for several miles. They were finding the coastal climate much cooler than the hot mountain valleys. Dust, grime and sweat coated the skins of the weary runners, but grit and determination kept them on their feet.

When nearing Crescent City on Monday, June 20, Mad Bull was six miles ahead of Flying Cloud and Melika six miles behind him. Fighting Stag was still in fourth place. There was no change in the running order as the marathon runners hit the Smith River Canyon with its curvy uphill mountainous roads. After several more grueling miles the end of the longest marathon in history was about to become a reality."[8]

"To cut to the chase, as they say, let's forward to the finish line, in Grants Pass, Oregon, where a skinny, young Karok from Happy Camp on the Klamath River outdistanced his younger brother by 10 miles, and the heralded Melika by 30 miles. Johnny Southard, running as Mad Bull, won the race in 7 days, 12 hours and 34 minutes. His record leg was 79 miles in 25 hours."[9] "He was carried about on the shoulders of the Oregon Cavemen and given an ovation. The street was thronged with thousands of persons who literally went wild. Mad Bull received his $1,325 in prize money and two hours later had bought a new car for $1,050 cash. He immediately took his mother and Little Fawn for a ride down Main Street.

Flying Cloud was second; Melika third, and Fighting Stag fourth. Rushing Water finished at fifth and Thunder Cloud sixth. Melika was the only Zuni to finish the race as Chochee had followed Jamon in retiring from the race."[10]

"Promoter Pyle had an equally good run. Flocks of reporters followed the runners through the redwood forests. Photographers proved hazardous to the runners as they jockeyed for the perfect shot. Reporters stormed the telegraph offices. In the time the runners were on the road, the news services averaged 300 words a day about the race—and the new highway. The Indian Marathon was the first-ever 'media circus' on California's North Coast.

The race was so successful they did it again in 1928. This time Flying Cloud was the winner and Melika, the Zuni grandfather, was second. It was to be an annual event. But the stock market crashed and there were no tourist dollars in the Great Depression that followed."[11]

Note: In addition to the California counties, Josephine County, Oregon, is among the Redwood Empire Counties. This explains why Grants Pass was selected as the Marathon's finishing point. "Rules specified contestants must be backed by a city, county, club or other organization. Each sponsor was to provide an automobile to carry an umpire and supplies for the runner. All contestants were to travel on foot, walking, running and sleeping at their own convenience. There was a requirement that each runner be at least one-quarter Indian. The first to reach the tape at Grants Pass would receive $1,000 cash while the next four would receive their share of another $1,000, additional prizes were to be awarded by some of the cities along the route." (Quote same as footnote 8 & 10.)

[7, 9, 11] *"Indian Marathon Touted Redwood Highway" by Gaye LeBaron, The Press Democrat, Aug. 8, 2004.*
[8, 10] *"1927 Race Tough Test of Stamina" by Evelyn McCormick, The Humboldt Historian, July-Aug. 1987.*

Heading north from Klamath make a left turn at **Requa Road** *(8.0) just before Minot Creek. This winding little road takes you to the* **town of Requa...the Requa Ferry...and the Requa Inn***. Just before climbing the hill into town there is a camp-ground to the left and the ferry was located down here about 100 yards upriver from the Requa Inn. When the ferry was still running this is where you would have arrived after crossing the Klamath River. Once the Douglas Memorial Bridge was opened in 1926, the highway bypassed Requa. However, the Klamath/Requa Inn remained a popular stopping place for travelers on the Redwood Highway.*

REQUA

Requa Road

"A gleaming white inn, several aged houses, and a sunny hillside cemetery mark the sites of two earlier, larger communities: the substantial Yurok village of Rek-woi and the clamoring cannery town into which it was transformed. Modern Requa got its start in 1876 when Martin Jones and George Richardson began catching and salting fish near the old Yurok village; Jones added a sawmill five years later. Next came R. D. Hume of Gold Beach, Oregon, who sailed a scow down to the townsite, built a structure on it, and opened a waterborne general merchandise store and salmon saltery. Soon dairy farms dotted the fertile bottomland east of town.

By 1909 booming Requa boasted a post office, store, hotel and feed stable, blacksmith, a few dwellings, and 'two places for satisfying the unnatural thirst.' Salmon canneries were the big business in town. A whistle announced the start of each day's fishing, and supervisors watched closely as derby-hatted fishermen boated their catch; when the observers calculated that there were enough fish to keep the cannery running for the rest of the day, the whistle blew again and the fishermen quit. The daily quota often ran to as many as 7,000 to 10,000 fish, a figure sometimes reached in only one or two hours. During salmon season, entire Yurok families left their upriver homes to come fish the lower Klamath or to work in the canneries. Commercial salmon fishing was banned on the Klamath in 1934. Once the canneries closed, the lower river became dominated by sport fishermen."[12]

The large building on the right is the Klamath Inn (later the Requa Inn). On the left are Thurston & Butler General Merchandise and a sign for a restaurant.

Irl Rickabaugh   TOWN OF REQUA   Late 1920s

[12] *Redwood National & State Parks – Tales, Trails, & Auto Tours, Jerry & Gisela Rohde, 1994.*

REQUA FERRY

Margarite Cook   REQUA FERRY   Mid-1920s
The section on the end is the ferry, the other section is a loading ramp.

At one time, a ferry was the only way to cross the Klamath River. The earliest travelers in pioneer times actually had to rely on the Yurok Indians who ferried them across in redwood canoes. In 1876, a toll ferry operated by Morgan G. Tucker was put into service. How quick passage could be made depended upon the tides. High water or extremely low tides could cause a delay of many hours.

A county wagon road was completed in the late summer of 1894 between Crescent City, Klamath and points south. Stages were then operating between Crescent City and Eureka. With the increase in traffic, a bigger and more reliable ferry was needed. William Bailey and Charles Fortain obtained a franchise from the county to operate a ferry across the Klamath River in 1895. Bailey proposed to run a 1,700-foot cable across the river and succeeded after several attempts.

"In 1919 Dave Ball and Ralph Carr received a contract from the Board of Supervisors to build a new ferry boat that was wider than any used before and could carry up to three cars while the earlier model had a capacity of only two cars. A gasoline engine was installed on the upper side of the boat. The engine turned a drum that held four turns of a light cable that was stretched across the bottom of the river and an end was anchored to either shore. One drive pulled the ferry across the river in one direction. By reversing the drive, the boat traveled across in the opposite direction." [13] Frank Bosch was operating the ferry when it went out of business in 1926 – the year the Douglas Memorial Bridge was completed.

Travel on Ferry 1921-1922	
5,306	- autos & trucks (not including mail & passenger stages 943 & freight trucks 54)
171	- horse vehicles
119	- saddle horses, pack mules or other pack animals
8	- bicycles
1,842	- pedestrians

Del Norte Triplicate – Feb. 23, 1923

[13] *Ferries on the Klamath by Ralph Hughes, Del Norte County Historical Society Bulletin – March 21, 1978.*

PIONEER INN – BAILEY'S INN – KLAMATH INN – REQUA INN

The first Requa hostelry was built in the early 1880s by David Leishman and called the Pioneer Inn. "In 1895 John M. Miller purchased the inn which at that time was the first stopping place on the road to Humboldt County, a distance of 25 miles from Crescent City. He moved the building from the lower side of the road and made additions to it to accommodate ten guests."[14]

W.T. Bailey who was manager for the Klamath Packing and Trading Company purchased the inn from James Otto in 1900. Bailey leased it out and Mr. & Mrs. Frank Thurston were running the place when it was destroyed by fire in August of 1914. Actually, it wasn't just the inn that burned, although that is where the fire started. Lost in the fire were Brizzard's and another store, a livery stable, dance hall, several homes and both of the town's saloons. Before the end of the year Bailey had rebuilt a 10,000 square-foot, 28 room structure at a cost of $4,000.

KLAMATH INN
Capt. & Mrs. Wm. Crone
Requa, California
$1.50 day up without bath
$2.50 day up with bath

Redwood Empire Assoc. - 1926

The inn was purchased by Else Laron in 1948 and renamed the Requa Inn. Larson operated it for around 30 years closing in the late 1970s. There were several other owners for a few years, then the inn closed and remained vacant until 1985 when Paul & Donna Hamby purchased the building, restoring and remodeling the entire structure. The Requa Inn was sold in 2002 to Dave and Barbara Gross and is still serving the traveling public.

The Requa Inn is the only commercial building remaining in Requa.

Irl Rickabaugh   *Sign says: REQUA INN Formerly Klamath Inn*

Note: These early establishments may have gone by different names, Pioneer Inn or Pioneer Hotel and Bailey's Inn or Bailey's Hotel.

[14] *Written by Esther Ruth Smith, Del Norte County Historical Society.*

POSTCARDS

This book would not have been possible without the photographic postcards that were taken from the 1920s to the 1950s. At one time, these postcards were affordable mementos purchased at tourist shops for five cents. Photographs were taken of motels, hotels, towns, vistas and tourist facilities not to mention every unusual tree, natural landform and turnout along Highway 101. Today, there are an extensive number of people collecting vintage postcards as a hobby and for investment. These five cent postcards can now sell anywhere from a few dollars to several hundred. The most important part of these postcards, however, is the story they tell of a vanishing landscape.

It you were to travel up and down the highways of Northern California revisiting these old sites, you would be astonished and disappointed to find that many of these places are now gone. They were victims of highway expansion, changing social habits and economic progress. We are fortunate that through the vision of early postcard photographers the memory has been saved for future generations.

One of the best, most popular and prolific photographers was Frank "Patterson". The Patterson Studio was based in Medford, Oregon from 1924-1928 and at one time, employed eight workers. In 1925, Mr. Patterson claims to have sold more postcards than any other scenic photographer in the west. With the redwoods becoming more and more popular he moved his business to Santa Rosa, California in 1929. He was known to pack up his car with camping gear for a photo taking mission and head out on the road for a week or more at a time. Getting close up and personal with the objects of his photography may be the reason his photographs were considered some of the best. Patterson's postcards of Northern California cover the time frame from 1927-1940. His postcards are all identified by a "Patterson, "Pat" or "Patt" in the lower corner of the postcard.

"Art-Ray" Pictures produced beautiful redwood tree photos that were very popular with tourists all over the United States. These postcards covered the time frame from 1935-1950 and were sold in gift shops, drug stores and sporting goods stores throughout the area. The business was owned and operated by brothers, Charlie and Leslie Payne. Along with their mother, they lived in and operated their business from a large travel trailer that they used to travel all over Northern California. They were a familiar sight along the Redwood Highway until they settled in Crescent City in the early 1950s.

Alexander J. "Zan" Stark was from Mill Valley, California. His attractive postcards cover the time period from the 1920s to the early 1950s under the name "Zan" of Tamalpais. He was also the official photographer for the Redwood Empire Association from 1937–1947.

Robert "Laws" of San Jose bought out Frank Patterson's photography business in 1944. He took his own photographs from 1946-1955.

Harwood operated out of Medford, Oregon and sold some of his cards to Patterson when Patterson was first getting started. Harwood stayed in business from about 1926 to 1940 and covered from the Columbia River to Santa Cruz. Some of his cards say "Harwood" and a lot have a "H" in a circle.

"Sawyers" was from Portland, Oregon. He took photos of street scenes and redwoods from the early to mid-1930s to 1941. Sawyers began producing postcards in the 1920s and they (the Sawyers Company) invented the View Master which is still sold today.

Note: Names that are underlined are used by the photographers to identify their postcards.

After leaving Requa we are back on today's Highway 101 heading north.

HUNTER CREEK

Nov. 1928

HUNTER CREEK OVERFLOWING COUNTY ROAD (Redwood Highway)
The original road may have run a little closer to the hillside than today's Hwy. 101.

*Courtesy of California Department
Department of Transportation Library*

CAMP MARIGOLD

Camp Marigold is still a familiar sight on the east side of the Redwood Highway. It has been in business since the late 1920s or early 1930s.

> 1936 – *Best Camps Assoc.*
> Camp Marigold
> 3 ½ miles NORTH of Klamath on U.S. 101. Store – Meals – Tent Space – Laundry – Fishing Nearby

> 1940s – *National Auto Club*
> 10 frame cottages, each with shower, toilet, kitchen and car shelter. With bedding and linen, $2.25-$2.50, house-car space – 50 cents. Open April to November.

> ## CAMP MARIGOLD
> ### ON THE AVENUE OF THE GIANTS IN BEAUTIFUL DEL NORTE COUNTY
> ### REX and HELEN AYARS, MGRS.
> ### REQUA

*Klamath River Sports Carnival
Souvenir Program – 1950*

Circa 1930

CAMP MARIGOLD

Building behind gas pumps is the office-store and burhls are advertised. On the left side of the gas pumps is another row of cabins that are not shown.

Irl Rickabaugh

WOODLAND VILLA

Irl Rickabaugh   *WOODLAND VILLA*

Mid-1930s – *Redwood Empire Assoc.*
Woodland Villa
Forty acres of scenic beauty located 17 miles south of Crescent City. Modern cabins, separated from one another to give absolute privacy for each cottage. See the famous Cathedral Tree. The modern cabins each have toilet and shower and offer every modern convenience.

1949 - *Redwood Empire Assoc.*
Woodland Villa
Twenty modern housekeeping cottages, 4 miles north of Klamath on Hwy. 101, between the famous Klamath and Smith Rivers, 1.25 miles to the ocean beach. A real vacation spot. Grocery store and gas station. Sensible rates. Cooking utensils extra.

Irl Rickabaugh   *WOODLAND VILLA*   *Late 1930s*
Art Schoenrock - Owner   *Bakery - Groceries*

GIANT REDWOOD PARK – BIG TREE PARK 10.50 Hwy. 101

Irl Rickabaugh   *GIANT REDWOOD PARK*   *1926*
Notice all of the camping gear attached to the cars.

1926 – *Automobile Club of So. California*
Giant Redwood Park
Name of Campground – GIANT REDWOOD PARK
Nearest Town or City – 6 miles north of Requa on
   Redwood Highway.
P.O. Address – Requa.
Capacity – 100 cars.
When Open – May 1.
Kind of Shade – Redwoods.
Remarks –- Tents, furnished or unfurnished, store,
   dining room, shower baths, camp stoves,
   community house.

GIANT REDWOOD PARK

"No trip over the Redwood Highway is complete without a stop over at Giant Redwood Park.

This beautiful park comprises fifteen hundred acres of redwood trees and ocean beaches. Here is found the largest redwood tree in the world, according to Mr. A.D. Lee, the manager.

Trips are made through the park, under capable guides, who explain all the wondrous growths peculiar to the redwood country.

The park is equipped to care for all types of travel.

Giant Redwood Park is sixteen miles south of Crescent City, California, and nine miles north of Requa."

Redwood Highway Review – Sept. 24, 1926

"Whereas, the name of the Redwood Highway has proven to hold a lure to the motorists of the state and nation, and

Whereas, the adoption of the name Redwood in connection with this traffic route has had a paramount effect on the success of the route and the vast territory through which it runs, and has become a definite and considerable asset to the State of California, and

Whereas, it was A.D. Lee of Del Norte County, California, who conceived the name for this scenic route, now therefore

Be it resolved, that the Redwood Highway Association in annual meeting at Petaluma, October 24th, 1925 spread upon its records due recognition and appreciation of said A.D. Lee for his happy thought in giving this route its name."

"Redwood Highway"

Del Norte County Historical Society

Redwood Highway Review - Nov. 1928

Jarl deBoer

Entrance to the park was on the Redwood Highway through the arches. The arches are still there today.

Sign on the building:
Hungry?
now serving
BREAKFAST
LUNCH-DINNER
Moderate PRICES

Jarl deBoer   BIG TREE LODGE   1940

About 1938 – Big Tree Park
25 cabins, hotel plan only, one and two rooms, bedroom, private bath. Rates: for 2, $1.50 and up; for four, $4.00 and up. Lunch 50 cents. Dinner 75 cents and $1.00 or a la carte. Five miles from the Klamath River for fall fishing. Big tree, 97 feet in circumference, 32 feet in diameter, 300 feet tall, within 100 yards.

(Norman Coulter owner in 1931.)

Irl Rickabaugh   CABINS AT BIG TREE PARK

WONDERLAND PARK –
WONDERLAND REDWOOD MOTOR LODGE –
WONDERLAND PARK TREES OF MYSTERY –
TREES OF MYSTERY

You can't miss this spot on the road. Still in business after 75 years, nothing else in this area compares with its formidable history as a roadside attraction. Started by Carl Bruno on 40 acres in 1931 as the Wonderland Park resort, it consisted of a small rustic concession building and cabins on the east side of the highway frontage, and a gas station across the road on the west side. "After laboring to survive the Depression, Bruno took on partner Carl Lewan in 1939 and then sold out to him in 1941. Lewan called the resort the Wonderland Park Trees of Mystery, named individual trees, and stayed with the business through the lean years of World War II before selling to Ray and Marylee Thompson in 1946."[15]

Everflowing Fountain, dedicated to the travelers of the famous Redwood Highway – Wonderland Redwood Park, Requa, Calif.   *Zan 601*

Irl Rickabaugh   *You can still see the fountain standing in front of the Trees Motel today.*

"THE BEST—IN REST—FOR EVERY GUEST"
WONDERLAND PARK
YOUR HEART'S DESIRE—PRIVACY—LOTS OF COMFORT—SECLUDED COTTAGES—PRIVATE ROADS—SCENIC TRAILS—MUCH TO DELIGHT AND THRILL YOU—THE GUESTS JUST HATE TO LEAVE THIS PLACE.

The Humboldt Times - Sept. 14, 1933

[15] *Journal Society for Commercial Archeology, Fall 1998.*

Jarl deBoer   WONDERLAND REDWOOD MOTOR LODGE

1935 – *Shell Directory*
Wonderland Park
4 ½ miles north (Klamath). Deluxe, apartment-like cottages, rugs, overstuffed furniture. Hot and cold running water, heated by steam, gas or oil. Electric or gas stoves for cooking, many have refrigerators and radio. Restaurants and grocery usually convenient. Open garages. $2.00-$6.00.

Jarl deBoer   REDWOOD CATHEDRAL TREE

Courtesy
Dave Parish

Ambrose Gruenke hitched his way up the Redwood Highway in the 1930s carving as he went. In 1938, he carved the "End of the Trail" sculpture out of a single, huge redwood trunk using only an ax, handsaw and knife. He left his name written out in nail heads on the horse's neck. The carving is a replica of the "The End of the Trail" sculpture by James Earl Fraser who was commissioned by the Pan-American Exhibition in San Francisco in 1915. You will find the sculpture located directly in front of the gift shop.

Trees of Mystery is still owned and operated by the Thompson family (now in its 3rd generation). Today, there is a new motel on the west side of the road where the gas station once stood. Cabins that housed travelers over the years are no longer available. The property has expanded to 120 acres and new trails have been built.

One of the older trails features unusual redwood growths, trees with names like *Upside Down Tree*, *Candelabra Tree*, *Family Tree* and *Elephant Tree*. The *Trail of Tall Tales* with a Paul Bunyan theme was completed in 1962. That same year a brand new gift shop was opened.

The *End of the Trail* Native American museum opened in 1964 and is free. It is one of the largest privately owned collections of Indian artifacts on view to the public. Marylee Thompson has spent over 50 years assembling this collection and her goal is to protect and preserve this heritage for future generations.

The *Kingdom of Trees* trail brings you in touch with coastal redwoods, Sitka spruce and Douglas fir along with informational displays and audio presentations. Just opened in 2001 is *Sky Trail*, a gondola ride through the redwood forest canopy to an observation deck with spectacular views. The Thompson family is proud of their business and legacy. The secret to their success is that they are always adding to the place and who knows what the future holds in store.

Early 1950s

Babe the Blue Ox is 35 feet tall -- Paul Bunyan is 49 feet 2 inches tall.

Courtesy of the Clarke Historical Museum

SEE THE FAMOUS

Trees of Mystery

—FEATURED IN—

RIPLEY'S "BELIEVE IT OR NOT"
AND UNIVERSAL NEWSREEL

"STRANGER THAN FICTION"

NATURE'S GREATEST SHOW!
You've Never Seen Anything Like It!

A TREE OF MYSTERY

SEE THE WORLD'S LARGEST REDWOOD
CATHEDRAL TREE—105 ft. around, 320 ft. Tall
AND 7 OTHER BIG TREE WONDERS
SEE DEER IN THEIR NATIVE HAUNT
FOLLOW THE SIGNS TO THE

GIANT REDWOOD HORSE

The Trees That Made the Redwood Highway Famous

Irl Rickabaugh

Postcard text:

The
SACRED TREE
of the
REDWOODS

This is their temple vaulted high,
And here we pause with reverent eye,
With silent tongue and awe-struck soul,
For here we sense lifes proper goal.

To be like these, straight, true and fine,
To make our world like theirs a shrine;
Sink down, oh traveler, on your knees,
God stands before you in these trees.

Jarl deBoer   ENTRANCE LOG AT TREES OF MYSTERY PARK, REDWOOD HIGHWAY, KLAMATH, CALIF.

1947 – The first Paul Bunyan statue was made for a Victory Garden Parade in Southern California. It was made of paper mache.

1948 – A second statue of Paul Bunyan was made after the rain and weather ruined the paper mache one.

1950 – Babe the Blue Ox statue made.

1962 – Current Paul Bunyan statue completed. It is the largest animated statue.

Jarl deBoer   *OCTOPUS TREE*

Del Norte County Historical Society   LOGGING TRUCK ON REDWOOD HIGHWAY

LOGGING AND THE HIGHWAY

During World War II demands for lumber instigated the development of the vast, virtually untouched, fir timber resources in Del Norte, Humboldt and Mendocino counties. New areas were opened and mills of all sizes and production capacities were developed in areas only served by state and county highways. Previously, the redwood industry had used logging railroads to transport trees from the woods to the mill and sent their finished products by railroad and ship. It wasn't long before logging and lumber trucks became an important segment of the traffic traveling on the highway and helped to show the glaring deficiencies in the old road system. Normally, the heaviest traffic on the Redwood Highway had been in the summer months with recreational and tourist traffic. Now, with the expanding timber industry, highway usage was up year round. The population also doubled at the same time. At that time (early 1950s), it had already become apparent that the Fortuna-Eureka-Arcata area would need a four-lane highway and plans were being developed. However, it now became necessary to review the plans to cover the entire length of the Redwood Highway in Del Norte, Humboldt and Mendocino counties.

Courtesy of   *California and all the West*   *1951*
Joe Leger   ***BY GREYHOUND*** ®

Permission for use by Greyhound Lines, Inc.

NORTH TO CRESCENT CITY

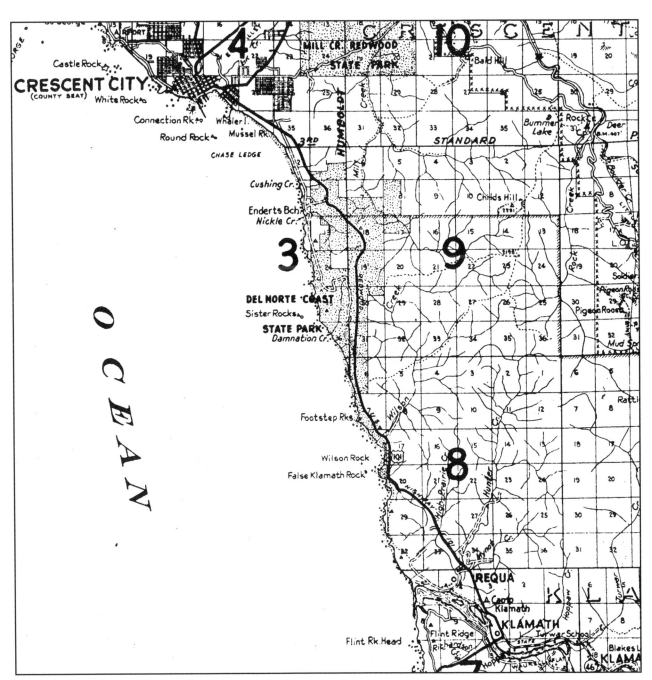

Courtesy Metsker Maps/Janssen Inc.   *DEL NORTE COUNTY - 1949*

De Martin Beach.
The only place where
the Redwood Highway
comes down to the water
963. PERSON

Irl Rickabaugh   *TRAVELING THE REDWOOD HIGHWAY*   *Late 1920s*

NEW SPAN OPEN
Del Norte's First Four-Lane Expressway

"The date February 10, 1957, marked the opening to public traffic of Del Norte County's first section of four-lane expressway. The yet incomplete project on US 101 extends from 0.1 mile south to one mile north of Wilson Creek, which is approximately 12 miles north of the Town of Klamath.

The new facility, a 60-foot, all paved section providing for four-lanes, is 1.13 miles in length, including a 282-foot reinforced concrete box girder bridge over Wilson Creek. This facility shortens the distance between project termini approximately 0.5 mile and replaces a portion of US 101 constructed in 1924, which combined the very undesirable elements of narrow roadway, heavy grade, short radius curves, and restricted sight distance. These factors accounted for a relatively high accident rate with 68 accidents recorded within the limits of the project for the period 1940 through January of 1957.

With the opening of this section of expressway, the elimination of 'Dead Man's Curve,' a 125-foot radius curve at the bottom of a sustained 6 percent grade, came as a welcome relief to the drivers of the many heavy commercial vehicles traversing this route. Failure to maintain air in brake lines, fading brakes, and the ever-present menace of heavy fog have each taken its toll of vehicles and drivers."

California Highways & Public Works, March-April 1957
Courtesy of California Department of Transportation Library

OCEAN VIEW TERRACE

Irl Rickabaugh   *OCEAN VIEW TERRACE*

*Notice the gas pump on the front porch. The banner hanging
over the front of the porch advertises Golden Shell Motor Oil.*

Irl Rickabaugh   *OCEAN VIEW TERRACE*   *1932*

Mid-1930s –
*Redwood Empire
Assoc.*
Ocean View
Terrace
Eight miles north
of Klamath.
Beautiful marine
view from clean
roomy cottages
with good beds.
Coffee shop in
conjunction
serving excellent
food to order.
Near state
redwood parks.
Convenient to
fishing the
Klamath River or
ocean. Rates,
unfurnished
$1.50 up;
furnished $2.00
up.

*Buildings still there
in the 1960s.*

THE OLD COUNTY ROAD

"The supervisors of Del Norte County authorized the construction of a road from Crescent City southerly to Requa, on the Klamath River, to connect with a road from Eureka, some 65 miles to the south. This road, placed under construction in 1889 and completed six years later, permitted the first vehicular travel from Crescent City to Requa, at that time a thriving fishing and cannery town.

Transportation by Rowboat
Prior to the construction of this road, freight consigned to Requa was received at Crescent City by infrequent lumber schooners and unloaded into large rowboats, which were then rowed by as many as sixteen oarsmen down the coast to the Klamath River and thence to its destination. Mail destined for Crescent City was received by boat at Eureka, hauled to within six miles of the Klamath River and then packed on horses to the river. A rowboat transported it to the opposite shore where it was once more loaded on horses and packed to its destination over beach and mountain trail, a trip which in the stormy season required days to make.

Upon completion of the Crescent City-Requa road, stages drawn by four or six-horse teams were placed in operation. A fare of $5 was charged and the trip required ten to sixteen hours, dependent upon the weather. The old landmark called 'Tubs Spring,' near the road now under construction, was the stopping place for watering the horses as well as the lunching place for the passengers. In 1910, an automobile touring car replaced the horse-drawn stage, though the lack of rock ballast frequently required the use of the stage teams to pull the auto stage through the many deep quagmires. This resulted in the trip often taking hours, whereas now it is made in thirty minutes.

As travel increased, the necessity for some type of surfacing became apparent. Timber being plentiful and readily available, puncheon—planks hewn or split from redwood trees—were placed transversely to the road and served the purpose. This construction though insuring a stable road surface, resulted in the roughest riding surface conceivable; a ride over it never to be forgotten.

Eventually, the greater portion of this road, within timbered areas, was surfaced with puncheon which at the present time shows little deterioration from its original condition. No difficulty is encountered in driving over the portions of the road in Graves Park. This road, though now relegated to the past, is to be maintained in its original condition as an interesting means of comparison between an old and a new highway.

The construction of a State highway between the county seats having been provided for by the Highway Bond Act of 1909, a highway between Wilson Creek and Crescent City was constructed and opened to traffic in 1920, resulting in the abandonment of the puncheon road that had served the citizens of this section for so long."

California Highways & Public Works – March 1934
Courtesy of California Department of Transportation Library

ON THE OLD
COUNTY ROAD
*The Road surface
was redwood
puncheons (planks
hewn or split from
redwood trees).*

Courtesy of California Department of Transportation Library

*REDWOOD
HIGHWAY
Mid-1920s*

Irl Rickabaugh

*REDWOOD HIGHWAY
Circa 1929*

Irl Rickabaugh

Touring The Old Redwood Highway

AUTO STAGE ON THE REDWOOD HIGHWAY   *1933*

TWO STATES JOIN IN DEDICATION OF RELOCATED REDWOOD HIGHWAY SECTOR

"With picturesque pageantry in which present day leaders of California and Oregon joined with descendants of early pioneers, costumed Indians and Oregon 'Cavemen,' the recently completed sector of the Redwood Highway (State Route No. 1) in Del Norte County, south of Crescent City, was formally dedicated on Sunday, August 18th (1935).

The reconstruction of this nine-mile sector between Last Chance Slide and Flanagan's saves eight-tenths of a mile in distance and eliminates 205 sharp and dangerous curves totaling 9,557 degrees of curvature or about 26 ½ complete circles. The savings to motorists in operating costs, conservatively estimated at 30 cents per vehicle trip.

Seven miles of this nine-mile section follows closely along the top of a ridge parallel to the coast from 600 to 1,100 feet above the ocean, through a dense virgin redwood forest. Three miles of this area lies within the California State Park System, where the forest will be preserved in its natural state. The old road also traverses the park area at a lower elevation where it will be maintained and serve as a park road. The entire (new) roadway has been surfaced with 9 to 12 inches of crushed rock and provision made for successive applications of oil as required.

Several large slides have occurred which have brought the total excavation to in excess of 700,000 cubic yards. These slides have been removed for a safe distance from the shoulders. They continue to move, however, and no doubt will be a considerable factor in maintenance cost for a few years. But the soil is such that they will gradually cease to move and will not become the perpetual menace and source of expense encountered along the so-called Crescent City Bluffs or the old highway.

The new road leaves the forest area five miles south of Crescent City at an elevation that affords a panoramic view of the Smith River Valley and the rugged coast line for many miles toward the east and north."

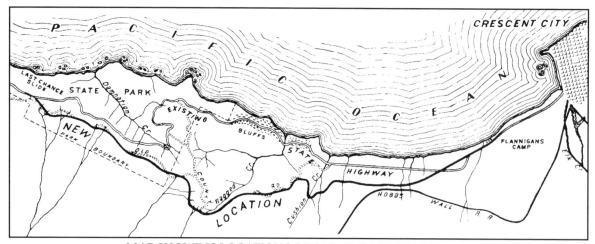

MAP SHOWING LOCATIONS OF OLD AND NEW HIGHWAY.

California Highways & Public Works – Sept. 1935
Courtesy of California Department of Transportation Library

CONSTRUCTION OF REDWOOD HIGHWAY SOUTH OF CRESCENT CITY
With garden tools, an ax, a team of horses, and strong backs, widening of a turn in the road is attempted. The highway wanders through the woods taking the line of least resistance. The season in which these men were working was pleasant, but when the weather became wet the road became a guagmire.

Courtesy of California Department of Transportation Library

Slide in Summit Cut. Making road that slid between Wilson Creek and Crescent City in 1935.

Both Photos: Courtesy of California Department of Transportation Library

Construction Last Chance Slide to Flanagans - South of Crescent City - 1934

Joe Leger REDWOOD HIGHWAY Late 1920s or Early 1930s
The original highway along the bluffs south of Crescent City.

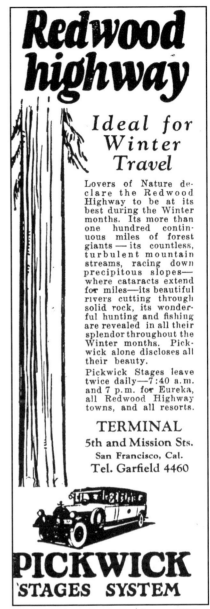

Redwood Highway Review - 1928

A BIG RUSH COMING

"Contractors will finish the last stretch of the Redwood Highway this fall.

The spring of 1929 will see a broad scenic drive, unsurpassed by any drive in the world.

From 700 to 1,200 cars a day are going through now. No matter what kind of car you drive, you can have an easy journey.

The big Pickwick and Southern Pacific stage make schedule time from Grants Pass and San Francisco to all points on the Redwood Highway."

Redwood Highway Review – Oct. 1928

Courtesy of California
Department of Transportation Library

CLEARING FOR TRAFFIC WHERE ROAD SLID INTO OCEAN

1925

Del Norte County Historical Society
The Highway is either being constructed
or this is one of many slides.

Courtesy Sandra Nuss
Harry Parks working on the highway about 1924.

*Coming out of the redwoods and down the hill into **Crescent City**, shortly after it levels out, you need to make a left turn on **Enderts Beach Road**. This road was the original Redwood Highway that ran along the bluffs and was replaced in 1935. At the end of the road (2.2 miles) Redwood National Park has a parking area and an overlook. If you stop at the overlook and take a look south you can still see sections of the old highway carved into the bluffs.*

ENDERT'S BEACH

E - Enderts Beach Rd.

The cottages at Endert's Beach were located on a cliff-hugging section of the original Redwood Highway along the bluffs.

ENDERT'S BEACH
Fred W. Endert, Prop.
Crescent City, California
Rates on Application

Redwood Empire Assoc. – 1926

1926 – *Redwood Highway Assoc.*
Endert's Beach
Open all year. Capacity 40. Cottages,
Curios, Photos. Fred W. Endert.

*Endert's Beach still being
advertised in 1947.*

Irl Rickabaugh

Joe Leger　　　　　*ENDERT'S BEACH*

Irl Rickabaugh   THE REDWOOD HIGHWAY -- Crescent City is in the background.   *Early 1930s*

POZZI'S – CUSHION CREEK AUTO PARK   E - Enderts Beach Rd.

The Alexander/Pozzi Ranch is now part of Redwood National Park. Alexander started the ranch in 1869 and in 1914 the Pozzi family purchased it. They ran the ranch until the 1980s when it was taken over by the park.

1936 – *Crescent City Directory*
Pozzi's
Old highway south of town(4.3 miles) near beach.

The ad states that Pozzi's was 4.3 miles from town. The city limits changed over the years as the town expanded so this number can be misleading. This is true of all of the early town advertisements.

Del Norte County   CUSHION CREEK AUTO PARK   *Late 1920s*
Historical Society   *Located on east side of road near what is now Crescent Beach Picnic Area.*

CRESCENT CITY

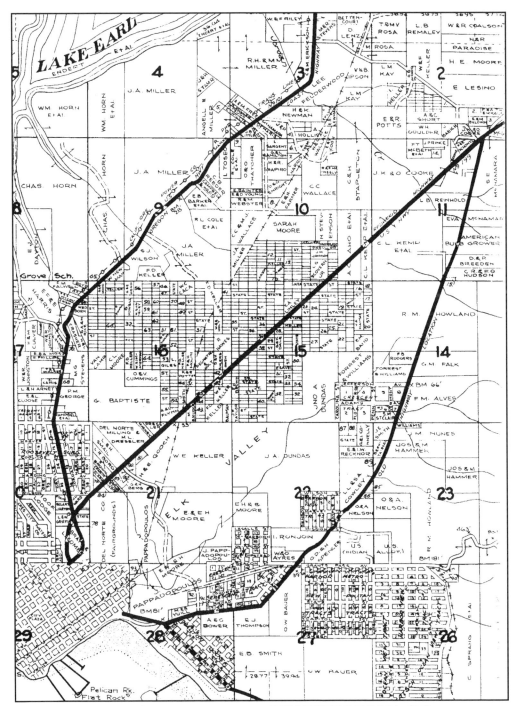

Courtesy Metsker Maps/Janssen Inc.   *DEL NORTE COUNTY - 1949*

*After taking a little side trip on Enderts Beach Road it is time to get back on **Hwy. 101** again. Across the road from the intersection of Enderts Beach Road and Hwy. 101 was the Oceanway Motel.*

OCEANWAY MOTEL

This is the first place you come across after descending the hill into Crescent City. Located right on the corner of Hwy. 101 and Humboldt Road, it has been there since 1950 and possibly earlier. In 2006 the business is closed and the buildings are still standing.

OCEANSIDE AUTO PARK – FLANAGAN'S AUTO CAMP – GAMMON'S CRESCENT BEACH CAMP – CRESCENT BEACH AUTO CAMP

This is a particularly confusing spot since it changed names so many times. It started out with Oceanside Auto Park on the east side of the road and then became Flanagan's. Around 1938, the auto camp on the west side of the road was built. After this, it seems that the businesses on both sides of the road were combined. To confuse things a little more, there was another Crescent Beach Auto Camp that became Van's Auto Camp around 1935 (at another location). I have tried to figure this out as best I can but there is still some mystery here.

1926 – *Automobile Club of So. California*
Name of Camp Ground–OCEANSIDE AUTO PARK
Nearest Town or City – Crescent City
P.O. Address – Crescent City
Capacity – 12 cabins and open tent grounds.
Charge – 50 cents to $1.50 per day.
When Open – All year.
Kind of Shade – Trees.
Remarks – Located on level with ocean. 5 mile beach drive. Cabins with kitchenettes, running water, beds, etc. Hot and cold showers, laundry, fireplaces, community kitchen. Clams, crabs, deep sea fishing, bathing, also mussels.

1935 – *Conoco Travel Bureau*
Flanagan's Auto Camp
U.S. 101. 22 cottages $1.25-$4.50.

GAMMONS CAMP

Late 1930s

Irl Rickabaugh

Located on the east side of the highway across from today's Crescent Beach Motel. The old fireplace and fountain are still standing.

Irl Rickabaugh

CRESCENT BEACH AUTO CAMP
Located on the west side of the Redwood Highway. Built around 1938.

1954 – *Redwood Empire Assoc.*
Crescent Beach Motel
Located 1 mile south of Crescent City on Highway 101, this motel is directly on the water's edge overlooking the broad Pacific. Cool, restful, scenic setting on a 4-mile stretch of sandy beach. 25 modern units with individually controlled electrical heat. Single or large parties. For reservation phone 4-R-2 or write Box 441, Crescent City.

STAY IN DEL NORTE COUNTY, "THE COUNTY BEAUTIFUL"

"Del Norte County (the North County) is, as its name implies, the northernmost county in the state. Being isolated from the busy whirl of commerce, having no rail communications, and, in the past, roads that were nearly impassable, it has retained all the natural beauty and wildness of an undiscovered country.

Crescent City, the county seat, is at the north end of Crescent Beach, a five-mile stretch of smooth hard sand on which you may drive your car as fast as you dare. It is said that there is no speed law governing the beach. A breakwater, two small islands and the gentle slope of the sand eliminate all undertow and one may enjoy a swim with no fear of danger.

Five miles from Crescent City is Endert's Beach, where razor clams may be dug. Crabs abound in the pools left by the receding tide and surf fishing can be enjoyed at any time or tide.

The visitor at Crescent City should visit the following places without fail:

Pebble Beach, one mile west, where many beautiful agates are yours for the finding.

The million dollar breakwater which will make Crescent City one of the most prosperous cities in northern California.

Smith River, a delightful little dairy town."

Redwood Highway Review - July 6, 1926

CURLY REDWOOD LODGE

THE STORY OF THE CURLY REDWOOD LODGE

The Curly Redwood Lodge was built from one Curly Redwood tree and the Curly Redwood Tree was located where the airport now is, near the Klamath River.

The top had been struck by lightning at about 100 ft. and a large growth like burl was growing out of one side near the top. (Very good burl).

It was 18'2" at the butt cut and curly to the tip of every branch. It was so huge it had to be cut into 5 logs and quartered, then loaded over its own stump.

It was loaded over its own stump by smoothing the stump with a chain saw. One side was cut out just the height of a truck bed and three logs were put on the opposite side of the stump so the quartered logs could be pushed onto the truck bed with a caterpillar.

The logs were sawed by a local logging company and produced 57,000 board feet of lumber and then they were stacked to air-dry.

All the lumber and plywood companies in the area were very cooperative or the job could never have been completed.

Del Norte County Historical Society

The Curly Redwood Lodge began as an idea by Tom Wyllie who owned the Redwood Room in Klamath, California. He thought it would be possible to build a lodge out of one redwood tree. The lodge opened in 1957 and the wood to this day is displayed inside and outside of the building. If you are looking for a unique, one-of-a kind place to stay, this redwood lodge definitely fits the bill.

Tom (Robert) & Lucile Wyllie owned the businesss from 1957-1964.

Dave Parish   CURLY REDWOOD LODGE   *Late 1950s*

DAVY JONES LARDER

Joe Leger

Only curly redwood shake ceiling in the world.

Circa 1940

Notice the unusual marine themed fireplace and the pinball machine in the corner.

davy   jones   larder
½ Mile South of   CRESCENT CITY, CALIF.   On 101 Highway
NEAR NEW AQUARIUM
A unique Seafood Restaurant....located on the shores
of the Pacific Ocean, in the Redwood Empire
_____

Crab, Shrimp or Olympia Oyster Cocktail..... 15c
Fresh Clam Chowder.....15c
Cracked Crab.....35c
Crab Louie........35c   Crab or Shrimp Salad...25c
Salmon Steak.....35c   Halibut Steak............35c
Steamed Littleneck Clams.....35c
Pacific Oysters, fried.....35c   Stew.....25c
CLAMBURGER ON A BUN...........15c
DELICATESSEN SERVICE

Arlene Hartin

1939

CRESCENT BEACH AUTO CAMP–VAN'S AUTO CAMP

Irl Rickabaugh   CRESCENT BEACH AUTO CAMP   Late 1920s

VAN'S AUTO CAMP
At Junction of Redwood and
Roosevelt Highways
* * *
Electrically Equipped Cabins
Store   Lunch Counter
Special Attention to Winter *Tourists*

MRS. MADGE ENDERT

Redwood Highway Review - Nov. 1928

1939 – *Shell Directory*
Van's Beach Cottages
South end Crescent City. 21 cottages, private toilets and showers, private cooking facilities, hot and cold running water in cottages. Garages with doors. (2) $1.00-$2.50; (4) $3.00-$5.00. Trailer spaces with electricity, public toilets and showers, 50 cents.

Irl Rickabaugh   VAN'S AUTO CAMP   1930s

THE BREAKERS AUTO APARTMENTS – THE BREAKERS MOTEL

Across from Elk Valley Rd.

Irl Rickabaugh

Late 1930s

1934 –
Shell Directory
The Breakers Auto Apartments Deluxe, apartment-like cottages, rugs, overstuffed furniture, hot and cold running water. Heated by steam, gas or oil; electric or gas stoves for cooking; many have refrigerators and radio. Restaurants and grocery usually convenient. Locked garages. $2.00-$6.00.

Radios - Steam Heat
Ultra Modern   **Phone 521**   Tile Baths
                                    Simmons Beauty Rest Beds

THE BREAKERS MOTOR APARTMENTS
ON THE BEACH

¼ MILE SOUTH OF CRESCENT CITY, CALIF.
Member of The United Motor Courts

Irl Rickabaugh

Irl Rickabaugh   *INSIDE THE BREAKERS*   *Early 1940s*

1951 – *Redwood Empire Assoc.*
The Breakers Motel
1/4 mile south (Crescent City). A motor court of distinction. 19 beautifully furnished carpeted units. Steam heat, radios, closed garages. AAA. Duncan Hines. Phone 521.

1954 – Kenneth D. & Wm. Virgil Hill hosts.

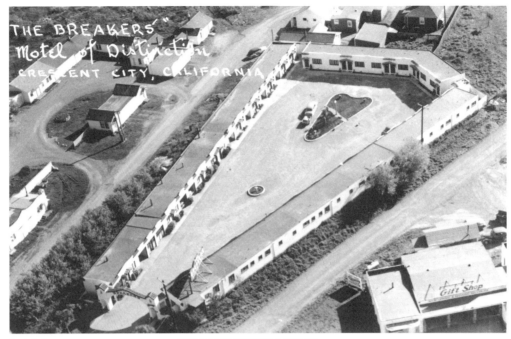

There were quite a few auto courts along this stretch of highway before entering downtown Crescent City.

Jarl deBoer THE BREAKERS MOTEL
The building on the right is the aquarium.

HARBOR AUTO COURT

Mike Knips HARBOR AUTO COURT 1941

Built in 1940

1940 – *American Automobile Assoc.*
Harbor Auto Court
1/4 mile south of Crescent City on U.S. 101. Daily rate 2 persons
– $3.00-$5.00. 14 cottages, private showers and toilets.

CRESCENT CITY AQUARIUM – SEA WONDERS ALIVE

Aquarium Opening

"The Crescent City Aquarium housed in a $15,000 stucco building located on the highway a quarter mile south of town, will open its doors to the public tomorrow morning. On display in tanks filled with clear ocean water may be seen many weird denizens of the deep secured along the ocean shore adjacent to Crescent City, including hermit crabs, different varieties of sea anemones, salt water eels, brilliant-hued starfish, small coral rocks and beautiful mosses and weeds.

Inside the aquarium, which has floor space 30 by 60 feet, are several large pools containing the fish specimens, starfish, octopus, sharks, cod and rock fish, sea trout and about 140 sea anemones which were taken from the ocean floor at a depth of about 300 feet. Some of the seaweeds shown are similar to desert cactus.

Built In The Walls

Over these large pools are twelve small tanks with round openings like port holes and equipped with indirect lighting which shows the exhibits to best advantage. In these tanks are living creatures taken from the sea, including many tiny fish which dart about among the rocks, small sea urchins, shells, snails, slugs, starfish, hermit crabs, barnacles, sea weed and pink coral. Some of these small specimens are so camouflaged by nature that they blend perfectly with their surroundings and it is impossible to distinguish them until they move.

The lighting fixtures for the tanks are so located that there is no glare in the eyes of spectators and every object in the tanks is in clear view at all times. In the outside pools will be exhibited sharks and seals.

The aquarium is supplied with salt water direct from the ocean through a four inch pipe pumped into the settling tanks which hold 60,000 gallons. The clarified salt water then circulates through the aquarium tanks insuring plenty of oxygen to the specimens on exhibition.

Some of the unusual specimens exhibited will be permanent, but for the most part the exhibit tanks will be supplied with new specimens so that patrons will find something new to attract attention each time they visit the aquarium.

The enterprise is backed by E.N. Berry and H.L. Collins, who have similar establishments on the Oregon Coast highway at Depoe Bay and Seaside, Oregon, and will be under the management of Mr. Berry. Mr. and Mrs. Berry will reside in the apartments built in the rear of the aquarium."

The Triplicate - April 28, 1939

*CRESCENT CITY
AQUARIUM*
On Highway 101   ¼ Mile South
Crescent City
The most unique and one of the most beautiful aquariums in the world. See the hideous octopus, the beautiful sea anemones and many other weird creatures from the ocean's depths living in glass front tanks and floor pools. Admission 15c, children 10c.

The Humboldt Times – July 2, 1939

Irl Rickabaugh   CRESCENT CITY AQUARIUM   1940

1956 – Sea Wonders Alive
On U.S. 101, just south of town. Marine Garden Aquarium and Gift Shop. Weird creatures living in clear crystal pools, amid beautiful rockery, deep sea plants, together with most interesting whale display on Pacific Coast. Also, largest, most complete gift shop on Redwood Highway. Hundreds of shells, Myrtlewood, Redwood gifts. Curios from all over world.

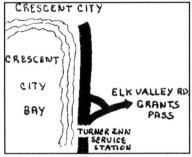

You can see that the intersection looked a lot different back then.

Lets take a little break here at Elk Valley Road. At one time, this was the Crescent City Turnpike (the pioneer stage road) to Oregon. It was also known as the Grants Pass Highway. In the 1920s it became the Redwood Highway. Today, if you follow this road till the end it comes out on the north end of Parkway Drive a short distance before the junction with Highway 199. This section of highway was used until around 1930 or a few years later.

Elk Valley Road was the junction for the Redwood Highway and the Roosevelt Highway. Travelers heading to Grants Pass made a right here on the Redwood Highway. Those wishing to take the Roosevelt Highway to travel to the town of Smith River or the Oregon coast continued north through Crescent City.

TURNER INN SERVICE STATION & AUTO CAMP

Irl Rickabaugh TURNER INN SERVICE *Circa 1930*
STATION & AUTO CAMP

TURNER INN
Junction Redwood-Roosevelt High-
ways, one-half mile south of
Crescent City
***
INFORMATION BUREAU
SERVICE STATION   LUNCHES
BUNGALOW CAMP

Redwood Highway Review – Nov. 1928

Early 1930s – *Redwood Empire Assoc.*
Turner Inn Service Station & Auto Camp
South entrance to Crescent City. Cheerful service
station service. Gasoline, oils, store, cabins.
Authentic road information.

(Copyrighted 1931 by Albert C. Turner)

TURNER INN
•
Coffee Shop
•
Richfield — Associated
Union
GASOLINE

Reliable Information

At Junction ½ Mile South of
Crescent City

U. S. Rte. 101 - Redwood Highway

TURNER INN
At Grants Pass Junction
ROUTES 101 & 199

½ Mile South of Crescent City
Ask for our Distance Card up Oregon
Coast Highway No. 101, or No. 199
to Grants Pass and Pacific Highway.

365—TURNER INN	0
5	
360—ENDERT'S BEACH	5
10	
350—WILSON CREEK	15
4	
346—REQUA JUNC. (1 mi. to Requa)	19
2	

Irl Rickabaugh

CYPRESS MOTOR INN –
PATTON'S CYPRESS AUTO COURT

Elk Valley Rd. & Howland Hill Rd.

Mid-1930s – *California State Auto Assoc.*
Cypress Motor Inn
Located 1 mile east of junction. Phone 23-X-1. 13 cottages, private showers and toilets, central sanitary conveniences. Housekeeping facilities, dishes and cooking utensils included, extra charge for bedding. Hot running water, well water, electric lights, wood heat. Camping permitted. $1.00 and up.

1949 – *Redwood Empire Assoc.*
Patton's Cypress Auto Court
Located two miles east on old Grants Pass Highway. Newly renovated throughout. Spend your time under the cool, shady trees. Grocery store and gas station. Reasonable rates. Ample room. No reservation required.

Mike Knips   *CYPRESS MOTOR INN*   Postmarked June - 1930

Located on the old Redwood Highway (Grants Pass Highway) – now Elk Valley Road.
The road on the left is Elk Valley Road and the road on the right is Howland Hill Road.
Cypress Motor Inn was still being advertised in 1949.

Sign on top of building:
FURNISHED CABINS
CYPRESS MOTOR INN
ASSOCIATED GASOLINE
CYCOL MOTOR OIL
Cabins   Groceries   Soft Drinks

REDWOOD HIGHWAY NOW IN GOOD CONDITION

"The improvements that have been made in the Redwood Highway are such that to us who have been using this route for years it seems that they are nearly perfect although the new road is not entirely completed.

The worst part of the route between San Francisco and the northern states has been eliminated with the passing of the old road over Oregon Mountain.

The highway between San Francisco and Eureka is in perfect condition. The speed law is thirty-five miles an hour and that is all one has to worry about. From Eureka to Grants Pass, Oregon is a different matter. It is far from being the worst road in the world though, and there is no reason why one should not make this trip. The following is the actual condition of the road at the present time, and this will be true until the first of October.

At Grants Pass, Oregon, the Redwood Highway turns off to the right from the Pacific Highway. From Grants Pass to Selma, 22 miles is excellent graveled highway. Selma to Kerby, 8 miles, will be cut upon till the first of Sept. owing to new construction. This road is in good condition except for numerous short detours around the new work. The next 45 miles is over the new highway which is wide, well graveled and smooth. There are three short detours on this stretch, none of which are over one-tenth of a mile.

From here to Douglas Park is over new highway just completed by convict labor. This road is a little rough but not bad.

The next 9 miles is through the redwoods to Crescent City and is in good shape always.

At Crescent City the highway turns south along the coast. For 16 miles it winds in and out along the cliffs, through massive redwood groves to Giant Redwood Park. This stretch of the highway is through the most picturesque and beautiful country along the coast. At no other place will such a diversification of scenery be found. Wonderful ocean vistas, beautiful giant redwoods backed by towering cliffs. This 16 miles of road is wide, smooth and graveled.

The next 6 miles to Requa is being widened out. The few sharp curves will now allow the passing of any sized car.

A new bridge at Requa will be opened to the public in a short time. At present a ferry that is well handled makes continuous trips across the river causing but little delay.

The road from Requa to Orick (25 miles) is in excellent condition. The 'chuck' holes and rough spots have all been smoothed out and this stretch is faster than it has ever been before. It has been widened out this year and there are few narrow spots left.

Arcata to Eureka (8 miles) paved.

Eureka to Scotia (30 miles) paved.

Scotia to Willits (111 miles) good, wide, smooth highway.

Willits to Hopland (36 miles) paved.

Hopland to Cloverdale (18 miles) good, smooth highway.

Cloverdale to Sausalito (85 miles) paved.

Sausalito to San Francisco by ferry (5 miles).

Oakland, Berkeley and East Bay points may be reached by ferry from San Quentin Point. San Quentin Point is about four miles from San Rafael."

Redwood Highway Review – Sept. 24, 1926

California by Motor Coach

The business man, the field worker, the vacationist, the week-ender, the tourist—all appreciate the fact that the pleasant and speedy mode of traveling is by Redwood Highway Motor Coach.

Each individual window can be raised and lowered at will, with separate smoking compartment for men. Automatic heaters and the latest ventilating devices insure your health and ease.

Drivers are obligingly courteous and always hold your personal comfort and welfare of first consideration. Rests and stops along the line are designed for your personal comfort.

It is cheaper to ride by stage than to drive your own car!

Economical rates now in vogue, with special round trip fares, mean substantial saving in your traveling expenses. It is far less expensive to travel in Redwood Highway Coaches than to drive your own automobile.

G Crescent City - Marshfield - Roseburg

North and East—Read Down West and South—Read Up

P. M.	A. M.	A. M.	Fares	Miles		STATIONS		Fares	P. M.	A. M.	P. M.	P. M.	P. M.
-----	9.00	7.00	$ 0	0	Lv	Crescent City	Ar	$11.50	8.00	-----	3.30	-----	-----
-----	7.45	7.45	1.00	-----		Smith River		10.75	7.15	-----	2.30	-----	-----
-----	11.30	8.30	2.00	30	Ar	Brookings	Lv	10.00	6.30	-----	1.00	-----	-----
-----	-----	11.45	6.00	70	Ar	Gold Beach	Lv	6.00	3.00	-----	-----	-----	-----
-----	-----	12.15	6.00	70	Lv	Gold Beach	Ar	6.00	2.45	-----	-----	-----	-----
-----	-----	3.00	8.50	100		Port Orford		3.50	11.30	-----	-----	-----	-----
4.45	7.00	4.30	9.75	130	Lv	Bandon	Ar	1.75	10.00	8.40	1.15	4.15	8.40
5.40	8.00	5.30	10.75	140	Ar	Coquille	Lv	.75	9.00	7.40	12.15	3.15	7.40
5.45	8.00	5.45	10.75	140	Lv	Coquille	Ar	.75	8.50	6.50	11.50	2.50	6.50
6.35	8.50	6.35	$11.50	170	Ar	Marshfield	Lv		8.00	6.00	11.00	2.00	6.09
5.00	11.00	7.00	-----	0	Lv	Marshfield	Ar	$5.00	12.20	5.50	8.30	1.50	3.50

B Eureka - Crannell - Trinidad - Orick -

North Bound--Read Down

Sun.	†34* Daily	No. 26 Daily	No. 28 Daily	No. 30 Daily	No. 6* Daily	32 Daily		STATIONS		No. 31* Daily	No. Da
p. m.	p. m.	p. m.	p. m.	a. m.	a. m.	a. m.				p. m.	p.
9.15	-----	5.00	1.00	9.15	9.00	7.00	Lv.	Eureka	Ar.	3.00	---
9.35	-----	5.20	1.20	9.35	9.20	7.20		Arcata		2.35	---
9.40	-----	5.25	1.25	9.40	9.25	7.25		Alliance		2.30	---
9.45	-----	5.30	1.30	9.45	9.30	7.30		Mad River		2.25	---
9 50	-----	5.35	1.35	9.50	9.35	7.35		McKinleyville		2.20	---
9.55	-----	5.45	1.40	10.00	9.40	7.40		Berg		2.15	---
10.15	-----	6.00	2.00	10.15	-----			Crannell		-----	---
19.20	-----		2.05					Little River			
10.25	-----	6.15	2.10	11.20	9.50	7.50		Moonstone		2.00	---
10.35	-----	6.30	2.20	11.30	10.00	8.00		Trinidad		1.40	---
-----	-----				11.10	9.00		Orick		11.25	---
-----	-----	* Does not carry			2.00	11.00		Requa		9.25	---
		local passengers.			4.00	12.30	(1)Ar	Crescent City	Lv(1)	8.00	---

California
Redwood Highway Coaches

TOURS **STAGES**

West Coast Transit Co., Inc.

CLYDE EDMONDSON, G. P. A.

San Francisco, 75 Fifth Street, Phone Garfield 4460

General Offices. 3rd and B Sts., Eureka, Cal.

Eureka, 415 Fourth St., Phone 422

Also all stage depots and terminals

Or Leading Travel Bureaus

Courtesy of Joe Leger   1925

LOG CABIN COURT

1937 – *California State Automobile Assoc.*
Log Cabin Court
South end of city on U.S. 101. No phone. 11 cottages. Private showers, private toilets, housekeeping facilities. Hot running water. Extra charge for bedding. Electric lights, gas stoves. Camping permitted. $1.50-$4.00.

Irl Rickabaugh   LOG CABIN AUTO COURT   *Circa 1940*
It was located across the street from Totem Pole Park.

PATTERSON'S POST CARDS

"The Frank Patterson postcard views of the Redwood Highway make a perfect picture log of the trip over this scenic route. Tourists should make sure of having a real record of this trip and purchase a complete set. They are on sale wherever good pictures are sold."

Redwood Highway Review - Oct. 1928

TOTEM POLE PARK & AQUARIUM
"Ocean Wonders Alive"

Irl Rickabaugh

TOTEM POLE PARK

Entrance to the park was through the log with the owl on top.

From a sign in front of "The Stump Motel:" This redwood, the largest ever felled in Northern California, was chopped down with axes, it being too large for the saws of that day 1888. Required three weeks to fall. 85 ft. circum. and 27 ft. in dia. at base.

Jarl deBoer

TOTEM POLE PARK

Late 1930s

Text from sign:
THIS STUMP of one of the Largest Trees ever fallen, was Taken out in Sections, Sawed Lengthwise to Hollow it Out, then Reassembled to Show the Large Size of these Monsters of Mother Nature's Making.

Jarl deBoer   THE STUMP HOTEL
Apparently, the Drive-Thru Stump was turned into the Stump Hotel.

Jarl deBoer   OCTOPUS STUMP AT TOTEM POLE PARK

The largest totem pole in the world - 120 feet high.

Irl Rickabaugh

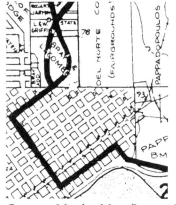

Courtesy Metsker Maps/Janssen Inc.
DEL NORTE COUNTY - 1949

Before we head into downtown Crescent City, it is time to go over the original highway route. It looked a lot different back then, when there was only one lane going in each direction. The highway came in on what is now **M Street** and made a left on **2nd Street**. Then it made a right turn on **H Street** and continued up to **9th Street** where it made another right. The road then continued out of town, heading north.

Today, 2nd Street deadends after a few blocks. It was changed after the 1964 tsunami destroyed most of downtown.

< North

Line through downtown added.

ROYAL MOTEL

Corner 2nd & L

1950 - National Auto Club
Royal Motel Built 1947. 8 modern units. $4.00-$6.00.

Del Norte County Historical Society   *ROYAL MOTEL*

TRAVELERS HOTEL

SE Corner 2nd & K

Travelers Hotel – Crescent City, Cal.

....On the Redwood Highway.. Noted for its hospitality and homelike atmosphere. Moderate rates and excellent meals.

Rates: Single $1.00-$1.50, with bath $1.50-$2.00. Double $1.50-$2.00, with bath $2.00-$2.50. Free garage. Coffee Shop in connection, serving meals at the following prices: Club Breakfast 25c, Lunch 35c, 4-Course Dinner 50c. We also serve all BRANDS OF BEER.

Overnight guests of the hotel are invited to enjoy a day of trout fishing, hiking, and swimming as our guest at our Lodge on beautiful Smith River, where you will be served a "DUTCH LUNCH" FREE.

The Humboldt Times - Sept. 14, 1933

The Aristocrat, Inc.
Courtesy Irl Rickabaugh

The Travelers Hotel was a stucco building with 36 rooms.

Early 1930s

NW Corner 2nd & K

Del Norte County
Historical Society

Early Crescent City Gas Station.
White building in background is the Traveler's Hotel.

1920s

1964 TSUNAMI

On March 27, 1964 a massive earthquake struck Alaska's Kenai Peninsula, heavily damaging Anchorage, located more than 60 miles away and sending a tsunami racing across the Pacific Ocean. Four tsunami waves would strike Crescent City. Today's tsunami warning system did not exist at this time. Most townspeople were home in bed and others were having a night out.

The first wave struck around midnight. Two hours later the fourth wave hit, it was the largest at a little over 20 feet. It was followed by a withdrawal of water that left the inner harbor almost dry. To add to the destruction huge logs laying on Crescent City's beaches from past floods acted as battering rams when the tsunami hit. Lumber, automobiles and other objects carried by the waves were responsible for a good portion of the damage to buildings in the area.

Dawns light showed unbelievable destruction. Twenty-nine city blocks were left in total or partial ruins. Crescent City's waterfront business district was gone and the devastation extended for about two miles south of the city limits. Automobiles, debris, and the ruins of buildings were piled in seaweed covered heaps. Eleven people were killed.

GARGAETAS AUTO COURT – EMPIRE AUTO COURT

1254 2nd St.
Between J & K

1949 – Redwood Empire Assoc. Empire Motor Court Complete ultra-modern, oil heated cabins. Located on 2nd St., U.S. Highway 101. Both house-keeping and hotel type. Hot and cold showers. Open all year.

Was in business in 1941 and possibly earlier.

Del Norte County Historical Society   EMPIRE AUTO COURT   1940s

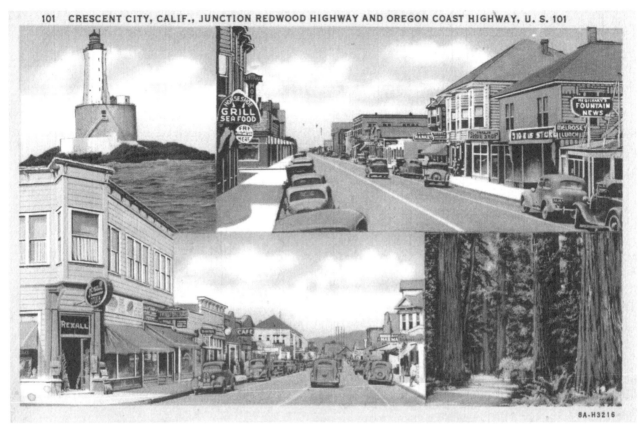

Arlene Hartin   CRESCENT CITY - 2ND STREET   *Late 1930s*

Del Norte County Historical Society   CRESCENT CITY - 2ND STREET LOOKING EAST   *Late 1930s*

Crescent City

Let's stop for a moment at the corner of 2nd & H Streets. Here on the southwest corner was the Bay Annex, an early hotel (post office today). A block south, sat the Hotel Lauff on the northwest corner of H and Front Street. This was the largest and most elegant hotel in Crescent City for many years.

Del Norte County
Historical Society

CORNER H & 2ND STREETS LOOKING SOUTH
Hotel sign on top right is Hotel Lauff.

About 1940

CRESCENT CITY

"The old circuitous highway route through Crescent City will soon be a thing of the past. Construction is under way from 0.7 mile south of Elk Valley Road through Crescent City and to 0.4 mile north of Northcrest Drive, a distance of 2.1 miles. This new routing through Crescent City includes a one-way couplet, with L Street serving southbound traffic and M Street northbound traffic. The typical sections include improvement of two-lane existing highway, four-lane street section, and four-lane divided highway, together with channelized intersections."

California Highways & Public Works -- July-Aug. 1958
Courtesy of California Department of Transportation Library

BAY ANNEX

SW Corner 2nd & H

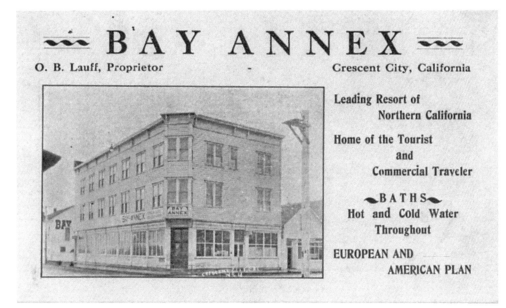

Irl Rickabaugh

1926 –
Redwood Highway Assoc. Bay Hotel and Annex Open all year. 40 rooms. $1.00 & up per day, $6.00 up per week. Hotel rooms. O.B. Lauff.

NW Corner H & Front St.

LAUFF HOTEL – HOTEL LAUFF – SURF HOTEL

Irl Rickabaugh   HOTEL LAUFF   1930
This whole area was changed after the 1964 tsunami.

Note: At one time this street was known as Ocean Drive. The name in the left corner of the postcard is incorrect.

Irl Rickabaugh

O. B. Lauff, as president of the Bay Hotel Company, began construction of the Lauff Hotel in 1926. It replaced an 1850s hotel on the Front and H streets site. Completed in 1928 at a cost of around $200,000, the five story concrete structure had 70 rooms. "It was the most elegant stopping place between Portland and San Francisco and played host to movie stars like Clark Gable, Carole Lombard and Hopalong Cassidy, and to governors and other notables of the late 1920s, 30s and 40s.

Lauff opened a large banquet room and coffee shop downstairs after World War II. In 1954, the Hotel Lauff was renamed the Surf by Orville Stump, the latest in a series of owners. Lloyd Bridges, Sr. of Eureka purchased the hotel in January of 1962. (Owned the Vance Hotel in Eureka.) He planned to return the hotel to its former glory, but died in a room at the Surf while negotiating with Buck Gurney who then operated the Hurricane Room. Gurney renamed it the Tidal Wave after the 1964 tsunami wrecked the downstairs. The Surf was left standing, while lesser buildings along Front Street were swept away.

The hotel had become a hot plate haven to the elderly and down-and-outers and was closed in 1974 because of the expenses involved to bring it up to fire standards. The forlorn-looking hulk stood vacant for 20 years, defying every attempt at rehabilitation by a series of hopeful owners."[16] The building was refurbished and made into apartments in the 1990s.

Joe Leger   *The hotel has dominated Crescent City's skyline for decades.*   *Early 1950s*

[16] *Written by Esther Ruth Smith, Del Norte County Historical Society.*

It was once a very classy place with a uniformed doorman and an elevator complete with operator.

Jarl deBoer HOTEL LAUFF LOBBY

J. L. WARD GARAGE

H Street

This garage was located on H Street two blocks north of the Hotel Lauff. Today, it is hard to imagine having a gas station in this area. However, there were several stations on 2nd Street, H Street and 9th Street when it was the Redwood Highway. A few blocks further north on H Street between 6th and 7th was the El Patio Motel that was built in 1949.

The Aristocrat, Inc. J. L. WARD GARAGE
Courtesy Irl Rickabaugh

Early 1930's –
Redwood Empire Assoc.
J. L. Ward Garage
2 blocks north of Hotel Lauff.
Complete garage service.
Storage, repairs, washing, lubrication, gasoline, oils.
Official A.A.A. Phone 500.
Reliable information on road, hunting and fishing.

CRESCENT CITY AUTO CAMP

Between 5th & 7th and D - F Streets

There is now a park at this location.

CRESCENT CITY AUTO CAMP

"Open the entire year, offers water, electric lights, wood at nominal cost and many other features to campers. The entire county of Del Norte is a natural camping ground—cool throughout the summer months."

Motor Land - July 1923

Joe Leger

Early-Mid 1920s

1926 – *Automobile Club of So. California*
Name of Camp Ground – CRESCENT CITY
  CAMP GROUND
Nearest Town or City – Crescent City.
P.O. Address – Crescent City.
Capacity – 150 cars.
Charge – Tent platforms 25 cents, cabins $1.00, camping 50 cents per car per day.
When open – All year.
Kind of Shade – Trees.
Remarks – Stoves, toilets, wood, lights, reading room, shower baths, wash room and ironing, hot water, some furnished cabins, tables, benches, children's playground, clamming, sea fishing, and agates.

BON DORME' MOTEL

NW Corner 9th & J

At one time, the Bon Dorme' (building on right in photo) was part of the Deluxe Auto Court.

1953 – Bon Dorme'
New, excellent $7.00-$8.00.

BON DORME' MOTEL   732 9TH ST.
"(Sleep Off the Highway)"

Del Norte County Directory – 1957

DELUXE AUTO COURT

SW Corner 9th & J

Irl Rickabaugh   DELUXE AUTO COURT   *About 1934*
The service station advertises STANDARD OIL PRODUCTS and REST ROOMS.

Mid-1930's – *Redwood Empire Assoc.*
Deluxe Auto Court
Located at the north end of Crescent City, within city limits, on Highway No. 101. 17 modern steam-heated apartments with all modern refinements including gas, electricity, hot and cold showers, cooking facilities, closed garages, privacy. Free use of lobby. Store and authorized Standard Station for your convenience. Rates $1.50 and up.

1959

PACIFIC MOTOR HOTEL

W - 440 Hwy. 101 N.

The building of the Pacific Motor Hotel was the wave of the future. This was a modern motel, with a lot of units, not a little mom-and-pop auto camp with a few cabins that were renovated over the years to accommodate the traveling public. New accommodations were being built with lots of windows, wall-to-wall carpeting, swimming pools and amenities such as telephones, radios and even televisions as time went on. Sadly, it was the beginning of the end, for the older auto camps who had a hard time competing.

PACIFIC MOTOR HOTEL   *Early 1960s*
Located across the highway from the county fairgrounds.

To Build New Luxury Motel (Built in 1956)
"A new luxury motel will be constructed at the north end of Crescent City by Kenneth and Wm. Virgil Hill, owners of the Breakers Motel here. The motel, to be called the Pacific Motor Hotel, will have 34 units plus managerial quarters and, planned for later addition is a restaurant and a liquor store.

Built of frame and masonry, with its ulta-modern lines sharply defined with lots of glass windows, particularly in the lobby, the motel will occupy 200 x 205 feet on 101 Highway across from the Del Norte County Fairgrounds. A flagstone fireplace will be in the lobby.

The Hill brothers said they are building it to 'rival the best in motel accommodations found anywhere on the coast' because they have faith in the future of Crescent City."

Del Norte Triplicate

HWY. 199 - ALONG THE SMITH RIVER

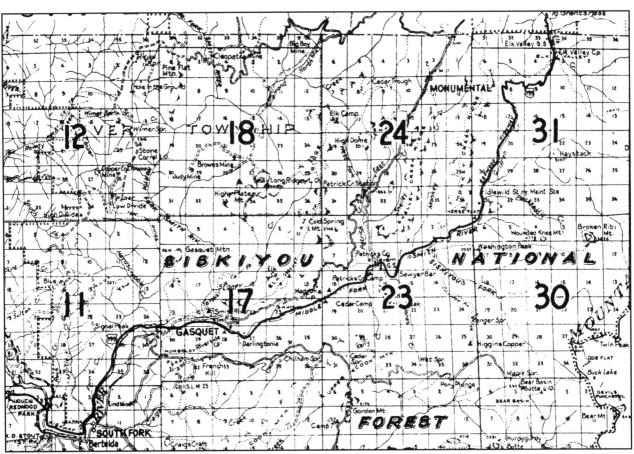

Courtesy Metsker Maps/Janssen Inc.   DEL NORTE COUNTY - 1949

Originally, there were only two choices at the north end of Crescent City. One route took you up the coast through the town of Smith River and towards Brookings, Oregon. To take this route, you would have taken Northcrest Drive, which was once known as the Roosevelt Highway. However, we will get back to this route later in the book.

*Right now we are going to head northeast on **Highway 199** along the Smith River. This is the Redwood Highway and it continued all the way to Grants Pass, Oregon. However, this journey is only going to take us as far as the Oregon border. To follow the old road when leaving Crescent City take a right hand turn on **Parkway Drive.** Parkway Drive was the Redwood Highway (Hwy. 199) from the 1930s until the freeway came through the area in the 1970s. Prior to that, Elk Valley Road was the Redwood Highway.*

*Follow **Parkway Drive** all the way to the end, and then make a right hand turn on **Hwy. 199**. Needless to say, all of the intersections at the beginning and end of Parkway Drive looked a lot different back then.*

TAYLOR'S MOTEL

> Parkway Drive

> 1952 – *Redwood Empire Assoc.*
> Taylor's Motel
> Modern, comfortable accommodations with or without kitchenettes. Located on 199 east of the junction, just beyond the north city limits of Crescent City. All units radio equipped. Orville and Thelma Christensen.

PAT & GUY'S CAFE

> 1 mile north on Parkway Drive

Irl Rickabaugh   *Opened for business in April, 1947.*   *1949*

REDWOOD MOTEL - East side of Parkway Drive just before Clyde Street.

ELITE MOTEL - 3160 Parkway Drive on west side, just past Elk Valley Road.

Irl Rickabaugh   *Early 1920s*

CONVICT CAMP TRANSFERS

"Plans are being made to transfer a portion of prison road camp, at work near the Klamath River, Del Norte County, to a new location on Smith River between Crescent City and Grants Pass."

California Highways - May 1924
Courtesy of California Department
of Transportation Library

THE REDWOOD HIGHWAY –
Early History of Transportation in the North Coastal Counties

"In the first 50 years or so of settlement in the north coastal region of California, few people gave thought to a north-south highway from San Francisco to the Oregon line. The Redwood Highway was not even a dream. Eureka, Arcata, Trinidad and Crescent City considered themselves seaports for freight to and from the Northern California valleys and the smaller towns near the coast depended upon these ports for export of their raw materials and import of their needs. Almost all the early settlement along the north coast in Humboldt and Del Norte counties was near the harbors where supplies might be landed from ships and transported inland to the many mines and diggings in the Klamath mountains. Today, hardly any of these early mining town sites are marked, and many are completely effaced; yet when they were operating, they required tremendous amounts of freight every week to keep them going. It all came in by sea.

Crescent City to Grants Pass

Although the northern end of the Redwood Highway, that section from Crescent City to Grants Pass, was not included in the state system until several decades after inclusion of the route from Arcata to Crescent City, it was a very important commercial route from the beginning. Crescent City, founded in 1853, for some time exceeded Eureka in freight tonnage, since it served all the Southern Oregon mines as well as most of the diggings in Siskiyou and Del Norte counties. In the early 1850s most of the freight went out on pack trains, up Cold Springs Mountain Trail. This was roughly the route of today's U.S. 199, although it veered a few miles east of the present summit. In these years sometimes 500 mules a week left Crescent City. Until the construction of the Southern Pacific Railroad in 1875 almost all of the freight for towns as far east as Yreka went through Crescent City, as well as a great deal of Southern Oregon supplies.

Mule Pack Train

In the Crescent City of the 1850s, mules were as common a sight as automobiles today. Pack trains were usually made up of 20-30 mules, which went out on the trail tied in a line. A typical train carried about 2 ½ tons. The packs held sides of bacon, bags of flour, kegs of whiskey, sugar, coffee, baking soda, matches, whale oil, lard, salt, frying pans, gold pans, nails, hammers, shovels, picks and ammunition, in the realm of necessities; and to the richer diggings almost anything a luxury hungry miner might want. There is a story that a piano was carried by a pack train from Crescent City to one mining camp gambling house.

Since a double freight wagon with an 8 or 10-horse team and driver could carry more freight than a 30-mule packtrain, the 'Crescent City Plank Road and Turnpike Company' was organized in 1854. Problems of financing and construction, as well as Indian wars, held up the road until 1858, when the first stage traveled over it from Oregon territory. This was a toll road, with tolls collected at the ferry over the Smith River. A two-horse team cost $5, a four-horse team $8, a six-horse team $10. The road was passable only from April or May until the return of wet weather, but a four-horse team could haul 3,000 to 3,500 pounds of freight 'over the hump.' By 1874 this road was in bad repair, and the citizens of Josephine County with difficulty raised $3,000 in taxes to fix up their end. The levy provided that taxpayers could pay or work out their tax on the road.

In 1882 a new toll road, the Wimer Road, was opened; started at the coastal end farther north, it followed roughly along the state line, but reaching eventually the site of Cave Junction, as all the other routes had. It bypassed a hotel operated by a Frenchman named Gasquet who, since 1877, had been operating a large traveler's inn part way up the Smith River Canyon, with French cooking, sleeping cabins, store, saloon, blacksmith shop, butcher shop, and many other outbuildings for poultry and livestock. In clearings nearby he raised corn, potatoes, table vegetables, fruit and grapes.

Gasquet Toll Road

Apparently to protect his investment, Mr. Gasquet in 1887 opened the Gasquet Toll Road, the best road so far, built with black powder and Chinese labor. It eliminated one of the worst features of the Wimer Road: a 1,500 foot drop into the canyon of the North Fork of the Smith and out again. The Gasquet route was essentially that of the present U.S. 199, except that near the summit it ran a few miles west until it crossed the Oregon line. It joined the future U.S. 199 at O'Brien and proceeded on to Grants Pass via Vannoy's Ferry across the Rogue River. Much of this road can still be traced through the rugged mountainous terrain.

On the Oregon side the commissioners of Josephine County did their best to keep the route serviceable. The county was too poor to build bridges over the numerous streams, but the commissioners took over issue of ferry licenses and levied a $3 fine if travelers were not taken in order of arrival. The ordinance stipulated priority was only to be given midwives and county commissioners. By the late 1880s, there was a bridge at Grants Pass over the Rogue, and stagecoaches left both terminus cities daily. There were 10-passenger coaches, with open sides and rolldown curtains. The body rested on six thick laminated leather straps four inches wide (thorobraces) which served as springs. The body was red and the wheels had two-inch wide steel tires. Four to six horses drew these vehicles at six miles an hour on the level, with loudly squeaking axles and towering clouds of dust. In 1900 the fare for the 200-mile trip from Crescent City to Grants Pass was $6.00.

In 1914 Frank Bosch put automobile stages on the Crescent City – Grants Pass run. These were two-cylinder International Harvesters with high wheels to cope with the ruts and ford the streams, and were designed with easily accessible parts for repairs and easily removable tires for replacement.

In the early 1920s the road was so much improved it was possible to make the trip from Crescent City to Grants Pass in 14 hours. An average of four to five miles an hour speed was good for substantial portions of the route. Stewart Mitchell, Jr., remembers traveling this road as a child, about 1923, in a Pierce Arrow stage which took all day to make the trip. Passengers stopped for lunch at O'Brien or Cave Junction, and arrived in Grants Pass after dark. The body of the stage stuck out a considerable distance beyond the rear wheels and on many of the sharp curves it was

Irl Rickabaugh　　　　　*FIRST AUTOMOBILE STAGE ON THE*　　　　*1914*
CRESCENT CITY - GRANTS PASS ROUTE

necessary to back up and turn to negotiate the curve. Stewart who was sitting in a rear seat, remembers looking over the side and discovering there was no road, only the cliff dropping sharply away beneath him.

The route became a state highway in 1927, and was realigned and paved within the next few years. In the early 1930s most of the old Gasquet route had been abandoned." [17]

OFFICIAL HIGHWAY GUIDE FOR DEL NORTE COUNTY

REDWOOD HIGHWAY—EAST—C. C. TO OREGON LINE— U S 199

.0 **SHELL SERVICE STATION** No. 689
   Myron W. Stevens, mgr.,
   9th and L Sts.,   1701
.1 County Hospital and Fair Grounds
.2 Junction U S 101—north
.2 State Highway Maintenance yard
1.3 Old Smith River-Crescent City R. R.
4.3 Intersection with Elk Valley Rd., turn right to Boy Scout Tree 31 ft. in dia.
4.4 Lincoln School
4.5 Turn left to Never Dying Redwood and U S 101
8.1 Hiouchi Bridge. Turn left on North Bank R. to U S 101
9.0 **EVERGREEN GLADE CAMP. Cabins, trailer and camping grounds.**
10.2 **RIVER BAR LODGE. (See inside front cover).**
10.3 Enter Smith River Canyon and scenic wonderland
11.1 Myrtle Creek Bridge
11.1 Turn right to Douglas Park, 2 mi., Stout Memorial Grove, California State Park System, 3 miles; Soldiers' Wells, 16.6 mi. and Rock Creek
15.1 Hardscrabble Creek bridge
10.0 Smith River bridge
16.2 Turn right, Big Flat, 31 mi., and Bear Basin
17.0 **SYMNS AUTO CAMP on Smith River. Cold drinks, lunches, store, fishing, swimming, service station, modern cottages, camp ground. Irene Symns and Frances Stevens.**
17.1 **MARY ADAMS STATION**
   Famous family style meals since 1896. Hot and cold showers, Good hunting.
17.9 Gasquet Camp, C. C. C.
18.5 Gasquet Ranger Station. Free camp fire permits. Hunting, camping and fishing information. Report fires in Nat'l Forest here. Phone connection.
18.5 State Highway Maintenance Yard
20.0 **DARLINGTONIA RESORT; 12 new and modern cottages, weekly rates. Fishing, swimming, golfing. The Darlingtonia, or insect eating plant on exhibition.**

21.1 Smith River bridge.
21.2 Eighteen Mile Creek bridge.
23.3 Cedar Forest Camp.
23.3 Smith River bridge
23.4 Madrona Forest Camp
24.1 Smith River bridge
26. Patrick's Creek Guard Station. Free camp fire permits. Hunting, camping and fishing information. Report fires in National Forests here. Phone connection.
26.3 **PATRICK'S CREEK TAVERN. First class all-year Hotel. Reasonable rates. Free Forest Service camp ground adjacent. Good swimming, fishing and boating.**
26.3 Patrick's Creek bridge, junction of forest road leading to old Gasquet and Wimer stage road, Diamond creek, Cleopatra Mines and Sourdough.
28.4 Smith River bridge.
29.2 Siskiyou Fork Trail, 6 ¼ miles to Bear Basin road.
30.1 George Washington Flat.
30.2 Monkey Creek Way Trail to old Wimer stage road, 8 miles.
32.5 State Highway Maintenance Yard
33.3 Horse Flat Way Trail
34.6 Oregon Mountain Way Trail
39.9 Hazelview summit, 2435 feet. This side of Oregon Mountain offers some of the most beautiful scenery in California.
42.7 Elk Creek bridge
42.8 Elk Valley Guard Station. Free camp fire permits. Hunting, camping and fishing information. Report fires in National Forest here. Phone connection.
43.3 **SISKIYOU MOUNTAINS CAMP**
   Hunting, fishing; a cool, quiet camp. Coffee shop in connection; store, service station and garage. Forrest T. Dunham, prop.
43.4 California State Quarantine Station
44.0 Oregon State line.
(Oregon Caves, 32 miles; Grants Pass, 44 miles; Portland, 322 miles.)

1941 - 1943

Note: Not all of the businesses are listed. Mileage has changed as the roads have been realigned over the years.

---

[17] *California Highways & Public Works, May-June, 1964. Courtesy of California Dept. of Transportation Library.*

Jarl deBoer   *REDWOOD HIGHWAY - HIOUCHI STATE PARK*

HIOUCHI BRIDGE

Irl Rickabaugh   *HIOUCHI BRIDGE*

"The latest member of California's state highway bridge family was officially dedicated on Saturday, June 22, 1929 when the Hiouchi bridge over the Smith River on the Redwood Highway was thrown open to travel. The occasion was notable inasmuch as it marked the completion of original construction throughout the length of the Redwood Highway, one of the great recreational highways of America.

Added interest was given to the completion of this bridge by the fact that just 100 years ago this same territory was explored by Jedediah Smith, who it is believed, gave his name to the Smith River. The route that it took months for the Jedediah Smith party to traverse is now traveled in a few hours time.

The bridge is a through cantilever steel truss structure, with a main span of 380 feet and two anchorspans of 114 feet, making a total length of 608 feet. The roadway is 24 feet wide. The contract price was $170,470.50, of which $149,925 was for the bridge and $20,554.50 was for approach grading and culverts. The floor of the bridge is 58 feet above low water. The bottoms of piers are approximately 20 feet below low water founded on rock. The total height from bottom of pier to top of steel is approximately 114 feet.

More than a thousand persons, gathered from all parts of the United States and included the governors of two states and many other notables, assembled at the Hiouchi Bridge at noon yesterday and rejoiced at the completion of the last major project needed to make the Redwood Highway a first class route from end to end."[18]

HIOUCHI BRIDGE ACROSS SMITH RIVER. U. S. 199 BETWEEN CRESCENT CITY AND PATRICKS CREEK. CALIF.   R64

MAIN SPAN 380 FEET CENTER TO CENTER.   44168

Arlene Hartin   *HIOUCHI BRIDGE*   *1938*
A new bridge was built around 1989-1990 after this bridge was damaged.

Located just east of the Hiouchi Bridge was a drinking fountain that was listed on maps and travel directories. These fountains were provided at intervals along the Redwood Highway by the Division of Highways. In the early days, vehicles overheated frequently and here was a place to stop and fill your radiator. Motorists also liked to stop, stretch their legs and enjoy some fresh spring water.

[18] *California Highways & Public Works – July/Aug. 1929.*
  Courtesy of California Department of Transportation Library.

For convenience, all addresses on Highway 199 will be given as north side or south side of the road, even though the highway runs northeast.

EVERGREEN GLADE

FISHING   HUNTING   SWIMMING

EVERGREEN GLADE CAMP
SERVICE STATION AND STORE
A.R. WOODWORTH, Owner
ON THE REDWOOD HIGHWAY   10 MILES EAST OF CRESCENT CITY, CALIFORNIA

Western Guide – 1930

Irl Rickabaugh   *EVERGREEN GLADE*   *Early 1930s*

1930 – *Western Guide*
Evergreen Glade
East 10 miles (Crescent City) on Redwood Highway. 8 cottages $1.50-$2.50. Bath, toilet, kitchenette, laundry, sleeping cabins, fuel, lights, water, bedding furnished, shade, playground, stream or lake, swimming beach, pool, fishing, hunting, guides, pack horses, boating, garage, service station, grocery, meat market, fresh milk, gas for cooking.

1949 – *Redwood Empire Assoc.*
Evergreen Glade
Presenting a complete tourist accommodation, located next to Mill Creek State Park, nine miles east of Crescent City. Clean units, kitchenettes, groceries, gasoline. Fishing, hunting, swimming. Open all year. Feel at home with Nell and Bob Home, owners.

Joe Leger   *EVERGREEN GLADE*   *Late 1960s*

Evergreen Glade was closing down because its lease expired when the building burned down on July 12, 1975. The Hiouchi Ranger Station is now located at this site.

HIOUCHI CAFE

S - Hwy. 199 - Hiouchi

This little business has been a fixture on the Redwood Highway since around 1933-34. No one seems to recall what it was named many years ago, but it has been known as the Hiouchi Cafe for quite a while now. At one time, there were around 12 cabins here and a cafe with two gas pumps in front. There were still two cabins standing and being rented out until the 1980s.

River Bar Lodge

ON HIGHWAY 199—10½ miles NE of Crescent City, Calif.

Modern Knotty Pine Cottages—On Smith River Out of Fog Belt

PHONE — "RIVER BAR"
FISHING
BOATING
SWIMMING
BADMINTON
PACK TRIPS

Irl Rickabaugh   *RIVER BAR LODGE*   *Late 1930s*
Notice the gas pump on the front porch.

1935 – *Conoco Travel Bureau*
River Bar Camp
Hwy. 199. 6 cottages, $1.25-$4.00.

1949 - *Redwood Empire Assoc.*
River Bar Lodge
Ten miles northeast of Crescent City, Hwy. 199 on the beautiful Smith River. Out of the fog belt. Swimming, boating, trout, salmon and steelhead fishing. Individual knotty pine cottages with all modern conveniences. Housekeeping and hotel accommodations. Shady lawns. Restaurant features home-cooked meals. Cocktails in our cozy lounge.

River Bar Lodge Open for Summer
"Jack & Florence Workman reopened River Bar Lodge last night for the summer season. The interior of the lodge has been renovated, floors refinished and chrome accessories added."

Del Norte Triplicate – May 2, 1952

Torn down around 1975-76. It was located across the highway from the Madrone Court Mobile Home Park at 2510 Hwy. 199.

Arlene Hartin   *SMITH RIVER AT FORKS*
        Notice the rock work along the road. This was done by the Civilian Conservation Corp in the 1930s.

11.95 Hwy. 199

Arlene Hartin   *This bridge across the Smith River was dedicated to Mary Adams Peacock in 1932.*

MUSIC BOX MOTEL

> 1952 –*Redwood Empire Assoc.*
> Music Box Motel
> Newly built cottages on the beautiful Smith River, 16½ miles from Crescent City on the Redwood Highway. Fishing information on trout, salmon and steelhead. Relax and enjoy this peaceful valley in all its grandeur. Cottages by day, week or month. For reservation, write Biff and Deddie Wold, proprietors, Highway 199, Crescent City.

WAGON WHEEL MOTEL

At some point in time, the Music Box Motel and the Wagon Wheel Motel combined and became one business.

Del Norte County Historical Society   WAGON WHEEL MOTEL   *Del Norte County Historical Society*

SYMNS AUTO CAMP

Symns Auto Camp in Gasquet was probably built in the early 1930s and was still in business in 1967 according to an advertisement in the West Coast Telephone book. Mrs. Irene Symns was the owner and operator of Symns Camp for many years. She was also the postmaster for the Gasquet Post Office.

Mike Knips

SYMNS CAMP
Frank Symns - Proprietor

Postmark May 29, 1933

1939 – *Shell Directory*
Symns Camp 18 miles northeast Crescent City. 8 cabins. Private toilets and showers, private cooking facilities, hot and cold running water in cottages. Shellane tank gas for cooking. Garages without doors. (2) $1.25-$3.50; (4) $1.75-$4.50. Trailer space with electricity, 75 cents a day. Trailer space without electricity, 50 cents a day. Public toilets and showers.

Jarl deBoer

SYMNS CAMP

*It wasn't until around the late 1920s or early 1930s that the Redwood Highway changed to the straight road that is used through town now. Before that the road followed what is now **Gasquet Flat Road (13.00)**. At the intersection of Hwy. 199 and Gasquet Flat Road sat Adams Station. You can still see a few old buildings if you make a left at this intersection. Following this road through the back of town (along the river) you would have also come across Horace Gasquet's Resort toward the other end of the road in the area behind today's Gasquet Store. This road brings you back around to Highway 199 but stay to the right when the road turns into the **Middle Fork Gasquet Road**.*

MARY ADAMS STATION – ADAMS STATION

NE Corner Gasquet Flat Rd. (13.00) & Hwy. 199 - Gasquet

Mary Adams came to the Gasquet Resort when she was a girl of about 20 years from Waldo, Oregon, where she was born in 1861. "She was born of sturdy pioneer parents, and, with the exception of a few years spent in San Francisco, the mountains have been her home. Since the early 1880s she has lived in the little valley on Smith River, and for a number of years she made her home at the Gasquet resort.

In the late 1880s at the suggestion of Horace Gasquet, Mary Adams homesteaded the 22 acres now known as Adams Station. Later she bought from Laurent Bonnaz, the flat and slope land, 100 acres, lying on the north bank of the river…at the same time Peter Peacock homesteaded 80 (*adjoining*) acres. Shortly, the Adams and Peacock homesteads joined lands when the owners joined hands in marriage. Already Mary Adams, first as manager for other stations and then as hostess of Adams Station, had endeared herself to thousands of travelers and tourists. Pete took to the station a Will Rogers humor and a fund of stories which added to Aunt Mary's culinary skill and sparkling wit, brought guests back to the station year after year."[19]

"When the hungry and tired passengers turn from the none-too-comfortable seats in the Concord stage to the thought of hot coffee and food and warm, soft beds, they thought of Mary Adams Station—in later years known as 'Aunt Mary's—where the drivers made their regular stops from Crescent City to Oregon points. The station wasn't just an ordinary station, a house with an ordinary yard. There was a special charm about them, perhaps as if they were a part of Aunt Mary, something different from any other house and yard. In the far end of the dining room, near the gold fish bowl and other furnishings given her by Horace Gasquet, was the register. It was not too large a book but in it every guest or visitor from the lowly to the famous, signed their name. Everyone registered. That was a rule of Aunt Mary.

Near ADAMS STATION RESORT
Mary Adams Peacock
Adams Station, California
Rates on application.

————

Redwood Empire Assoc.
Hotels & Resorts - 1926
Courtesy of Irl Rickabaugh

1926 – *Redwood Highway Assoc.* Adams Station Resort Open all year. Capacity 50. Old fashioned place. Mary Adams Peacock.

---

[19] *"The Old Woman Historian of the Mountains" written by Elp L. Musick in 1941 in the Del Norte Tripilicate. Later reprinted by the Del Norte Triplicate.*

The old road went by Aunt Mary's door, now US Highway 199. The wheels of stage coaches spit fire as they rolled over the graveled drive, warning the dogs and chickens and skunks to flee for their lives. The ways of travel changed but Aunt Mary's was ever 'the house by the side of the road.' Modern, stream-lined buses stood where the big-wheeled stage used to stop. She was still catering to guests with her cooking in 1941.

Part of the fun in going to Aunt Mary's for dinner was to visit with Uncle Pete. He used 'such' language. If we had used his words when we were kids, we would have been sent to bed. Coming from Uncle Pete those same words were happy bits of philosophy. If a tramp came to the door, usually escorted into the house by the dogs, when he left, if no one was looking, there would likely be a little jingle in the tramp's pocket.

Before the guests left the house by the side of the road, they would turn for one last look. It was good to have been there. Beside the big cherry tree they would see the spry, little old lady standing, the sun shining brightly on her glistening white hair, her eyes twinkling kindly. Pete stands at her side. The companion, tall, slightly bent, not from age but rheumatism. His shock of unruly hair, curled above his good-humored old face."[20]

Perhaps no other person in Del Norte County more truly symbolized the pioneer spirit of the West than Mary Adams Peacock, who passed away at her home in Gasquet, at the age of 81 in 1942.

The bridge across the Smith River near Aunt Mary's Station (page 98) was dedicated to the memory of Mary Adams Peacock in 1932. This bridge was replaced with a more modern one but still carries the original name. There is a plaque on the bridge by the turnout area. Also near the bridge is Mary Adams - National Forest River Access.

[20] *"Mary Adams: Pioneer Woman," by Ernie Coan (Mrs. Gordon Case gives a knowing pen picture of the celebrated couple). Del Norte Triplicate, Centennial Edition.*

HORACE GASQUET – GASQUET CAMP – VILLAGE OF GASQUET

Gasquet Flat Rd.
Gasquet

"In the summer of 1855, a little windjammer nosed into the bay at Crescent City. The passage around the Horn from France had been rough. Those aboard were tired, weary and seasick. Among them was a quiet young man who'd spent most of his life studying for the priesthood. That was not, however, to be his calling in Del Norte. Instead, he was to become an engineer, a road builder, a merchant, a farmer, and a mine and stage operator.

In January of 1857, he bought 320 acres of land on the north and middle forks of the Smith River. The town which bears his name lies 18 miles east of Crescent City on U.S. 199, on the original parcel. The first improvements on the property were done northeast of the current town site, but in a few months permanent buildings were erected on the present one. They included a hotel, bar, store, barn, blacksmith shop, winery and other small buildings. The town was the first settlement and stage station on the fringe of civilization northeast of Crescent City to become one of the noted resorts of the new west.

This French pioneer became a citizen in 1860. Sensing the unlimited possibilities in the virgin empire, he first applied his knowledge to the completion of one of the first mule trails to the interior and Oregon Territory. Over it he freighted thousands of tons of supplies and equipment to the interior mining camps and mines with his own mule pack train. He built another trail running down Gold Mountain to Indian Creek and Happy Camp on the Klamath River, where he opened another store. Also at Happy Camp, he started one of the largest mining claims on the Klamath. About this time he opened a store at Waldo, Oregon. His stores at Waldo, Happy Camp, his mining activities and road projects, as well as his farm were all handled with Chinese labor until the anti-Chinese legislation in 1886.

In the late 1880s life started speeding up on the frontier. For 20 years this pioneer had been freighting by pack mules over the old trail he had built from the Gasquet Station into Oregon and the Klamath River country. But this, he said, was getting to be too slow. So that he could send more freight at cheaper price to his stores and mines, he proposed the construction of the Toll road that was to make him even more famous as an engineer. He built his Toll road between 1881 and 1886. It ran for 20 miles from forks of the Smith up the middle fork to the state line between California and Oregon. Parts of the old road are still passable by car and make for a delightful Sunday drive.

Del Norte County Historical Society

ONE-THIRD MILE FRONTAGE ON SMITH RIVER

GASQUET CAMP ON THE REDWOOD HIGHWAY, CALIFORNIA   R.25

Dave Parish   *These buildings were part of Horace Gasquet's original resort. It was located in*
the area between Gasquet Flat Road and the current Gasquet Store on Hwy. 199.

In a statement filed with the Board of Supervisors in 1882, he asked to set these toll rates: footmen, each 25 cents; man and horse, $1; pack animals, ladened, 50 cents, unladened 25 cents; loose horses and cattle, 12 ½ cents, sheep, 6 cents; hogs, 6 cents.

The first and only bridge across the middle fork at the Smith River was completed by him in 1882. It was 105 feet long and 50 feet wide. It is seldom that one hears of a bridge folding up like a jackknife, but this one did just that, collapsing in July 1894 just after a mail stage had wheeled off the south approach.

In 1889 a heavy blow hit this pioneer. His wife died on November 27. Rapidly failing in health after her death, he was persuaded to enter a hospital at San Francisco. He died shortly afterwards in 1896 and was buried in Crescent City.

Gone today is the grape vineyard with its cultivated land and the orchard is no more and the winery with its many odors. None of the original buildings remain to mark the spot where thousands have stepped from a high-wheeled stage, while restless horses pawed the graveled drive. But the legend of Horace Gasquet endures. It lives in the town of Gasquet and in the mountains and the roads that felt the stamp of a unique and driven man."[21]

---

[21] *Del Norte Triplicate – June 25, 1983.*

Same buildings as photo on previous page, but from a different direction. Notice the cabins in the background. They were built after Gasquet owned the resort. In 1947, some of the Gasquet buildings burned and the remaining ones were razed in 1959.

The ad in the middle is copied from the back of the postcard on the opposite page. When they refer to the '50s in the text, they are referring to the 1850s.

Jarl deBoer   GASQUET AUTO CAMP

GASQUET CAMP ON SMITH RIVER

Hotel accommodations, Store and Filling Station.

Our cabins and camp grounds are situated on a one-third mile frontage on the banks of Smith River, in the midst of the original orchard, grape arbor and many other pioneer relics.

Our present community hall was built in the early '50s, at which time it was used to serve drinks to the original trailblazers of THE REDWOOD EMPIRE.

All of our cabins are equipped with running water and electric lights.

Public golf course adjoining.   Mrs. & Mrs. A.D. Rutherford, Proprietors

---

Irl Rickabaugh   GASQUET CAMP   *1930s*

1930 –
Western Guide
Gasquet Camp (on Smith River) 18 cottages, $1.50-$3.00. Bath, toilet, kitchenette, laundry, sleeping cabins, gas for cooking, lights. Water, shade, playground, stream, swimming beach. Fishing, hunting, guides, boating. Garage and service station, grocery, meat market, fresh milk. Watchman.

Joe Leger   VILLAGE OF GASQUET   1960s
Building in photo located on the NW corner of Middle Fork Gasquet Road & Hwy. 199.

The Village of Gasquet is a resort that includes 12 acres of land, a recreation hall, store and the old buildings that were part of the property of Horace Gasquet.

1949 – Redwood Empire Assoc.
Historical Village of Gasquet
A stage stop since 1852. 18 miles northeast of Crescent City on Hwy. 199, the Smith River Canyon Route. Our housekeeping cabins, clean and modern, are delightfully placed on the river. Tops in fishing. Cocktail bar and excellent food.

1950 – National Auto Club
Village of Gasquet
Built in 1947.
9 modern units. $4.00-$6.00.

IRENE SYMNS - NEW OWNER OF GASQUET VILLAGE

"Mrs. Irene Symns, owner of Symns Camp on Highway 199, on Wednesday of this week became the owner of Gasquet Village, having purchased the property from L.K. Shostak.

Mrs. Symns is well and favorably known to the residents of Del Norte County, having been the operator of Symns Camp for many years past and where she is Postmaster of the Gasquet Post Office.

Gasquet Village has an interesting history and is one of the oldest man-made landmarks in this county. Gasquet was established and named for the late Horace Gasquet away back in the 1870's. There he operated a general store, a hostelry and was one of the principal stage stops on the route between Crescent City and Grants Pass.

Following Mr. Gasquet's passing the property changed hands a number of times, finally being purchased by L.K. Shostak in 1944. Under his management, the store building was remodeled and a new reception hall and bar was added, and the name of Village of Gasquet was applied."

Source unknown

It is time to get back on Hwy. 199 after traveling on the back roads of Gasquet. Since we traveled around the back of town on the original highway, we bypassed the downtown area of Gasquet and the Gasquet Trading Post.

GASQUET TRADING POST MOTEL & CAFE

The Trading Post was owned by Joe and Ann Smith. There were six modern cabins at this location with a heated swimming pool. Home cooking and home-made berry pies helped draw in customers at the cafe. A slogan on one of their postcards states, *"In The Sunshine – Out of the Fog."*

The Trading Post was located on the highway just about in the middle of downtown. There are still some cabins there today.

*Sign on top of building:
Novelties
Coffee Shop
Groceries*

Mike Knips   Early 1950s

Greyhound takes you
THROUGH
World famous
REDWOOD
EMPIRE

1937

Mls.	404	SCHEDULE Nos.	405
		CRESCENT CITY—GRANTS PASS Table 21	
0	7 00	Lv EUREKA............Ar	5 45
84	9 51	Ar CRESCENT CITY.....Lv	2 45
	98	SCHEDULES Nos.	99
84	2 40	Lv CRESCENT CITY.....Ar	* 2 10
102	f	Lv Adams Station........Lv	f
103	f	Lv Gasquet.............Lv	f
111	* 3 32	Ar Patricks Creek Tavern. Lv	1 15
111	3 37	Lv Patricks Creek Tavern. Ar	1 13
129	f 4 19	Lv Cal.-Ore. State Line... Lv	12 31
142	4 33	Lv Caves City...........Lv	12 14
0	+	Lv Oregon Caves..⊕.....Ar	+
20	+	Ar Caves City...⊕.....Lv	+
142	4 35	Lv Caves City...........Ar	12 13
145	f 4 39	Lv Kerby..............Lv	12 09
151	f 4 49	Lv Selma..............Lv	12 00
164	f 5 06	Lv Wilderville...........Lv	11 43
174	5 20	Ar GRANTS PASS.......Lv	11 30

1937

*Schedule cover & schedule courtesy Joe Leger
Permission for use by Greyhound Lines, Inc. ®*

CIVILIAN CONSERVATION CORP (CCC)

In response to the Great Depression, President Franklin D. Roosevelt created many programs designed to put unemployed Americans back to work. The Civilian Conservation Corps (CCC), one of the first emergency agencies, was established in early 1933. Its mission was to reduce unemployment, especially among young men, and to preserve the nation's natural resources. This program was put on the fast track and from the time Roosevelt was inaugurated to the induction of the first enrollee was only 37 days.

The War Department was involved in the mobilization of men, material and transportation on a scale never before known in a time of peace. They were also responsible for operating the camps but the men were not subject to military control.

Responsibility for the selection and enrollment of applicants was under the Department of Labor. They were looking for young men between the ages of 18 to 25 who were unemployed and unmarried. Rules were eventually relaxed and unemployed veterans of WWI were also enrolled and at first housed in separate camps. Pay was $30 per month with $25 of that being sent home to their families by the government. This made life a little easier for people at home. Enlistment was for six months although many of the men reenlisted. Over the years, three million men would serve in the CCC.

Several federal and state agencies were responsible for coordinating work programs in our parks, forests, national monuments, wilderness and private lands all over the United States and its territories. The U.S. Forest Service administered more than 50% of all public work projects for the CCC. At its peak in 1935, the organization had more than 500,000 members in over 2,600 camps. California alone had more than 250 camps.

Some of the accomplishments of the CCC during its existence included 3,470 fire towers erected, 97,000 miles of fire roads built, over 4 million man-days fighting fires and floods, and more than 3 billion trees planted. They are credited with the development of more than 800 state and national parks, 4,000 historical structures, 60,000 buildings and 38,500 bridges. New roads were built and 89,000 miles of telephone lines were strung. There were over 500 camps involved in erosion control, many in the Dust Bowl, saving millions and millions of acres of land. Wildlife habitats were saved, streams restored, fish restocked and small dams were built for water conservation. Mile after mile of rustic rock fencing, walls and culverts were built using native rock and hand tools. Today, you can still see some of this beautiful rock architecture throughout the country. It has been written that it would take 50 years to accomplish what the CCC did in nine years.

By 1939-40 war clouds were on the horizon. Men were needed to fill jobs vital to the national defense. With unemployment down it became increasingly difficult to recruit men for the CCC. In July, 1942 the Civilian Conservation Corp program ended after nine years of service. There was still work to be done but national defense came first.

SISKIYOU NATIONAL FOREST – GASQUET RANGER STATION – SMITH RIVER NATIONAL RECREATION AREA

Traveling on Highway 199, you enter the Smith River National Recreation Area on the south end of Hiouchi. Much of the land from here to the Oregon border is part of the recreation area. The visitor center and headquarters (compound) is located in Gasquet right on the highway. It has a long history in the area.

It was in 1911 that Klamath's Gasquet Smith River Fork Ranger District was transferred into the Siskiyou National Forest. Siskiyou National Forest came into existence in 1906 and was part of Region 6 in Oregon. The first ranger station was located on the old county road (now Gasquet Flat Road near the school) until the 1930s. This section of road would become the Redwood Highway for a few years. These early stations were usually pretty primitive affairs.

A Civilian Conservation Corp (CCC) camp was established in Gasquet in 1933. I believe the camp was located near Wetherall Lane (13.86) about a half mile south of today's visitor center. Over the next seven years the CCC would be responsible for numerous improvements to the Siskiyou National Forest. The visitor center and the older part of the compound behind the rock wall (six buildings) were built by the CCC. Pine motifs on the visitor center are an Oregon design and it is the only visitor center in California with this design. Amazingly the compound has remained relatively intact and has retained its integrity. Known as the Gasquet Ranger Station, it is listed on the National Register of Historic Places. On the eastern side of the compound is a house built for a ranger and his wife by the CCC (now a barracks). It has a neo-Colonial design that actually comes from a home décor book and is not part of the national forest design.

The CCC were instrumental in developing the recreational campgrounds on the 199 corridor at Cedar Forest, Grassy Flat, Madrona, Panther Flat and Patricks Creek. Some of the many duties they performed were construction of lookouts, stringing phone lines, building and maintaining trails, planting trees and fighting fires. Numerous improvements were made to forest infrastructure. The Gasquet CCC camp was abandoned in 1940. They left an outstanding legacy.

In 1947 portions of Siskiyou, Klamath and Trinity National Forest became Six Rivers National Forest. Still part of Six Rivers, this area is known today as the Smith River National Recreation Area. The headquarters at Gasquet is one of the last intact U.S. Forest Service compounds in California.

Note: There was also a Civilian Conservation Camp at Big Flat near Hurdy Gurdy Creek on the South Fork of Smith River. It may have been an extension of the Gasquet Camp. This camp was probably responsible for Cooper Flat and Big Flat campgrounds.

FLOOD OF 1964

Rainfall around Christmas of 1964 caused one of the highest floods that the north coast had ever seen. The highway between Eureka and Crescent City survived fairly well except for the loss of the Douglas Memorial Bridge at Klamath and heavy flooding in Orick. "It was another story on U.S. 199 which carried the Redwood Highway into Grants Pass, Oregon, via the Smith River Canyon. Above Gasquet damage was severe. Three concrete arch bridges were carried away, and several miles of roadway lost. In places the roadway destruction here was so complete the canyon looked as though it had never had a road through it. So extreme was the damage in the canyon, it was days before it could be assessed adequately. Crews were sent up through Oregon to begin working on the northern end of the damaged area, and others started working from the south. The only way the damage could be surveyed properly over the 20 miles or so of worst devastation was by sending young engineers in on foot to hike through with backpacks. This meant miles of travel on foot through knee-deep mud, steep climbs high above the river through trackless forest to get around washouts, and sleeping and eating wherever local hospitality was available.

The bridge crossing Patrick's Creek had been destroyed and the contractor was authorized to build a log bridge until completion of already planned reconstruction of the road could be made on new alignment. Three miles south of here another bridge washout was replaced with a Bailey bridge.

In many places in the canyon reconstruction entailed virtually rebuilding the road, for where the rushing torrents struck the highway on outside curves, nothing was left. This required replacement of many thousands of yards of fill.

Partly rebuilt section of Route 199 in Smith River Canyon. Rock wall was for protection of fill but river rose much too high.

As on other routes, first movements were four-wheel-drive vehicles, followed quickly by convoys. As the bridges and the road were improved, the convoy system was extended. By Feb. 4, convoys were including passenger cars and single unit trucks with legal loads. Semis and trailers were excluded because they could not maneuver around the sharp turn leading onto one narrow log bridge. On the 14th of Feb. the road opened to all traffic on a 24-hour basis, subject to delay at construction sites.

On the afternoon of Monday, the 15th of March, representatives of the Greater Eureka Chamber of Commerce and the Chamber of Commerce of Del Norte County gathered at Klamath for a ceremony celebrating reopening of the bridge the night before. This was the last interruption in the roadway, and the Redwood Highway was once again a single entity." *

California Highways & Public Works - Xmas Floods 1964, Jan.-Feb. 1965
Courtesy of California Department of Transportation Library

* *There was still a detour at Rio Dell (Humboldt County) around the Robinson's Ferry Bridge until mid-May.*

RIVER VIEW AUTO CAMP – WHEELER'S RIVER VIEW AUTO PARK – NIELSEN'S RIVER VIEW RESORT

This auto camp was built in 1935 overlooking the Smith River. Today, it is hard to imagine there was ever a business on the riverside. However, the building site is actually under the freeway. When the new highway was built after the 1964 flood, the river was moved and fill was put in. The resort sat 10-15 feet lower than the road is now.

Irl Rickabaugh   *RIVER VIEW AUTO CAMP*

Mid-1930s –
*California State
Automobile Assoc.*
Riverview
Auto Camp
Located 19 miles
northeast on Hwy.
199. 8 cottages,
private showers
and toilets, central
sanitary
conveniences. Hot
running water,
spring water. Extra
charge for
bedding. Electric
lights, gas and
wood heat.
Camping
permitted. $1.00
and up.

Irl Rickabaugh   *CABINS AT RIVER VIEW AUTO CAMP*

1950–*National
Auto Club*
Nielsen's River
View Resort
10 modern units.
$4.00-$5.00.

*Smith River Lodge and Darlingtonia were on a piece of the old highway closer to the river. Today, this section of road is known as **Lado del Rio Drive.** The 1964 flood did a lot of damage in this area. When the roads were rebuilt after the flood, the new freeway was put in, changing the course of the original highway.*

SMITH RIVER LODGE

N - Lado del Rio Dr.

Smith River Lodge on the Redwood Highway 20 miles east of Crescent City. 160 acre playground. Coffee shop at popular prices. Attractive and comfortable. Redwood log cabins, reasonably priced. Excellent fishing, Swimming, hiking. 5 minute drive to golf course.

The Humboldt Times - Sept. 14, 1933

1935 – *Redwood Empire Assoc.*
Smith River Lodge
E. G. Thompson
Cabins are very modern and most attractive. Motorists stopping at Smith River Lodge are sure to be pleased. Deep sleep mattresses for your comfort. The Lodge is very attractive, and includes a coffee shop serving excellent food. Rates $1.00 to $3.50. Weekly rates; American plan. Write Smith River Lodge, Crescent City, California.

Irl Rickabaugh   SMITH RIVER LODGE   Early 1930s

DARLINGTONIA

Irl Rickabaugh   DARLINGTONIA   *Built 1935*

Darlingtonia was located toward the east end of the road. It was on both sides of the road with the gas station near the cul-de-sac on the river side.

Irl Rickabaugh   STAIRS TO THE RIVER

1954 – *Redwood Empire Assoc.*
Darlingtonia Cottages
Twenty miles east of Crescent City on the beautiful Smith River, fishing, swimming, hiking or hunting. Out of fog. Colorful wildflowers—native habitat of the famous Darlingtonia, or Cobra plant. Clean, comfortable cottages amidst woodsy setting. Some equipped for housekeeping. Restaurant within walking distance. Spend your vacation at Darlingtonia where our specialty is hospitality and friendliness.

Irl Rickabaugh   DARLINGTONIA CAFE   1940

FOREST PROJECT TO OPEN SMITH RIVER TO MOTORISTS

"The forest highway project now nearing completion on Smith River, in northern Del Norte County, with the work under way along the same stream by a prison road camp, soon will open to motor travel one of the most beautiful sections of California, a district now utterly unknown to most residents of the state.

The forest highway along the banks of the Smith River, in the Siskiyou National Forest, has a grade of about 1 per cent and winds through a canyon, the walls of which have an elevation of 2,000 to 5,000 feet. The present road climbs to this elevation, high above the river.

Many Beauty Spots
In the bottom of the canyon, never before accessible by a roadway, the engineers report a splendid growth of pine, cedar, oak and redwood. In many places, the canyon widens into little flats and other beauty spots by which Smith River, fed by springs, flows unabated during the dry summer months.

The highway has good alignment and averages about 21 feet wide. Of the 40 miles on the Redwood Highway between Crescent City and the Oregon line on the road to Grants Pass, 18 miles are under construction, 12 miles by contract and 6 miles by convict labor. In addition, 12 miles of grading has been finished and will be opened to traffic as soon as necessary bridges and surfacing have been completed.

Opening to travel of this 12 mile section, which probably will take place next summer, will eliminate Gasquet Mountain and greatly improve travel conditions between Crescent City and Grants Pass."

California Highways – January 1925
Courtesy of California Department of Transportation Library

PANTHER FLAT CAMP

This beautiful campground along the Smith River was built by the Civilian Conservation Corp (CCC) during the mid-1930s. It was once part of Siskiyou National Forest and is now in the Smith River National Recreation Area/Six Rivers National Forest.

Turn left at mile marker 17.02. This is a small stretch of the old highway with one of the last original bridges.

2005

Around 18.00 Hwy. 199

Jarl deBoer   *TRAVELING ON THE OLD REDWOOD HIGHWAY*   Late 1920s

CEDAR FOREST CAMP & GRASSY FLAT

18.87 Hwy. 199

This area was used as an informal campground by travelers even before it was a designated campground. It must have been a nice place to pull over and set up camp after traveling on the old winding road. Cedar Forest and Grassy Flat Camps were on either side of the Redwood Highway and across from Madrona Camp. Floods forced a change in the highway and campground layouts and the river was actually moved. If you drive into Grassy Flat today, at the end of the road is still a beautiful piece of the original highway bridge.

Located just north of Grassy Flat was another highway drinking fountain for travelers.

SIGN BUILT BY THE CIVILIAN CONSERVATION CORP (CCC).
Road on left is the Redwood Highway.

Both Photos: USDA Forest Service

CAMPSITE ON THE SMITH RIVER AT CEDAR FLAT

MADRONA PARK — MADRONA FOREST CAMP

There was once a beautiful rock wall and entrance booth at Madrona Forest Camp. The entrance and the camp were built by the Civilian Conservation Corp (CCC) in the mid-1930s. Part of the camp was lost in the 1964 flood.

Madrona Park Completed

"The Madrona Park project has been completed with the exception of a few finishing touches. The work progressed rapidly under the leadership of Albert Mosier, forest foreman in charge.

The park will accommodate fifteen or sixteen parties. The work of preparing the camp for occupancy consisted of building and graveling roads, building rock walls and abutments, and cleaning the camp site of down timber and debris.

This park is one of the many that will be ready for tourists of this region throughout the summer. It is sure to become a popular spot both to tourists and to local picnicers."

The Gasquet Gazette – March 23, 1935

Jarl deBoer　　　　*ALONG THE SMITH RIVER*

USDA Forest Service   *ONE MILE FROM PATRICKS CREEK*   *Late 1920s*

PATRICKS CREEK FORESTRY CAMP

S - 22.0 Hwy. 199

USDA Forest Service   *CAMPING AT PATRICKS CREEK*

At one time, Patricks Creek ran by the camp but the flood changed the course of the creek. Today, you see the Middle Fork of the Smith River touching the edges of the campground.

Forestry Camp, Patricks Creek.

Jarl deBoer

In 1934-35 the Civilian Conservation Corp and Forest Service built all the original structures at Patricks Creek Forestry Camp, including the entrance sign, register booth, bathhouse, toilet facilities, Siskiyou stoves, rock walls, the sculpted rock wall swim area (with diving board), and a rock-lined campfire area. Everything was made using natural materials such as rough-cut river stone or redwood planks, to blend with the environment. This made the camp a rustic and charming getaway that families have returned to year after year.

The campground suffered some of the district's heaviest losses in the 1964 flood. Lost were ten campsite units, considerable masonry work and the local swimming area. The ground underneath these improvements went down the river, making repair impossible.

Patrick Creek Swiming Pool

It is definitely worth the time to stop and see the beautiful stone masonry work that has survived in this beautiful setting. The kiosk in the parking area has some nice old photographs.

Irl Rickabaugh

PATRICK'S CREEK STAGE STATION – PATRICK'S CREEK TAVERN – PATRICK'S CREEK LODGE

"The Patrick's Creek Stage Station, which was located on the Gasquet Toll Road where Nine Mile Creek empties into Patrick's Creek, was established by George Dunn, Irish foreman for Horace Gasquet when the Gasquet Road was made. George Dunn built several cabins at this place about 1900. He was building a larger building when he was murdered by two young men who thought he had a lot of gold hidden in his cabin. They found $7.50.

After this tragic event, Lew Higgins bought the Dunn estate and finished building the station in 1906. The Higgins family operated this station of ten rooms until it burned and they built a larger place. On October 23, 1910, the Higgins family sold this station to Fred Raymond and sons, Don, Austin and Howard. Due to the charming hospitality of the Raymonds, this station became known far and wide as one of the most popular places in Del Norte County. It was over this old Gasquet Road, past Patrick's Creek Stage Station that Jack London and his wife drove their four black horses in a buckboard when they visited the county in 1911. This station burned in 1928.

When Redwood Highway (Hwy. 199) was open for traveling in 1926, the Raymonds built a new stopping place on the highway at the mouth of Patrick's Creek which they called Patrick's Creek Tavern. Opening night was May 8, 1926."[22]

"After 35 years of courteous service to their many guests, the Raymonds sold their place to Sam Wilson in 1946. Mr. Wilson remodeled the building, added a bar, and changed the name to Patrick's Creek Lodge. In 1947, the lodge was sold to Messrs. Tuttle, Renault, Piper, Fletcher and Wheeler

YOUR HOME ON THE REDWOOD HIGHWAY   R32

Dave Parish   *PATRICKS CREEK TAVERN*   *Late 1920s*
That is a Redwood Highway Tours auto stage in front.

---

[22] *Written by Lola Moore, Del Norte County Historical Society.*

with Fletcher and Tuttle later buying them out. During the 1950s, socialites from near and far dined, danced, partied, toasted festivities and even gambled into the night.

In the mid-60s, Ed and Elizabeth Becker purchased the lodge and kept it active through the late 70s. It then passed to two different owners up to 1986, then closed the winter of 1986 for two years and was abandoned. In the fall of 1988, Bill and Cindy Grier purchased the lodge and started reconstruction, opening in August of 1989. Open year round, the gentle hospitality of food and rooms and natural surrounding still awaits the traveler today."[23]

PATRICK'S CREEK TAVERN NOW OPEN TO PUBLIC

"One of the big events in Del Norte County this year was the opening on Saturday, May 8th, of Patrick's Creek Tavern. This beautiful hotel is situated half way between Grants Pass, Oregon and Crescent City, California.

The building, which is made of logs, is absolutely modern throughout. The rooms are plastered, have hot and cold running water and about half of them are equipped with baths. There is no better equipped hotel on the Redwood Highway.

The spacious lobby is comfortably furnished in rustic style, and has a beautiful fireplace which takes an eight-foot log.

Comfortable cabins are now being built and eventually a private campground and service station will be added. The forest service will maintain a large free camp beside the river, which will be one of the most beautiful places of its kind on the coast.

Fishing is always good in the numerous creeks and rivers surrounding the Tavern.

The Tavern is now serving tourists and local people at low rates and are still maintaining their unexcelled dining service.

The Raymond family have been taking care of the public in this locality for many years and have a wonderful reputation for service."

Redwood Highway Review - July 6, 1926

Irl Rickabaugh *PATRICKS CREEK LODGE LOBBY*

1935 - *Redwood Empire Assoc.* Patrick's Creek Tavern Management: The Raymond Family. A unique, modern hotel of log construction. On Smith River and Patricks Creek, in the rugged Siskiyou National Forest. Amusements include swimming, golf, horseshoes, croquet. Good trout fishing. May 1st to Sept. 1st. The dining room provides good meals at moderate prices. Also lunches.

[23] *Patricks Creek Lodge Brochure - USDA Forest Service.*

Patrick's Creek Tavern

See All of the Redwood Empire

Fruits, Juices and Preserves

Apple Sauce	10	Orange Juice	15
Fresh Berries (in season)	20	Sliced Orange	15
Grapefruit (half)	15	Fresh Peaches (in season)	20
Grapefruit Juice	15	Prunes	15
Melons (in season)	15	Tomato Juice	10

Jam, Jelly or Marmalade . 10

Canned Figs or Pears — 15

Fresh Crisp Cereals

With Cream — 20c

Kellogg's Corn Flakes   Pep 30% Bran Flakes
Wheat Krispies   Kellogg's Shredded Wheat Biscuits
All-Bran   Rice Krispies   Cooked Cereal
Wheat Krumbles   Kellogg's Bran Flakes

Eggs and Meats

Country Fresh Eggs (2) (any style except shirred) 30
Country Fresh Eggs (2) with Bacon or Ham 50
Omelet with choice of Jelly, Cheese or Ham 40 50
Plain Omelet 35   Ham or Bacon 45
Poached Eggs (Vienna) . 50

(Toast and Coffee served with above orders)

Griddle Cakes and Breads

Toast, Dry or Buttered	15	All-Bran Griddle Cakes	
Cinnamon Toast	20	with Syrup	20
French Toast	35	Griddle Cakes with Ham	
Milk Toast	25	or Bacon	40
Griddle Cakes with Syrup	20		

Hot Butter Ham — 10¢

Beverages

Fresh Hot Coffee	10	Ice Cold Milk	10
Hot Tea (pot)	10	Buttermilk	10

Hot Chocolate 10

• THE BETTER THE BREAKFAST, THE BRIGHTER THE DAY •

Courtesy of Patricks Creek Lodge   *Menu prior to 1946*

Irl Rickabaugh   *PATRICKS CREEK LODGE*   *After 1946*

1949 - *Redwood Empire Assoc.*
Patrick's Creek Lodge
This mountain resort will please you whether for a few hours or an entire vacation. Unexcelled steelhead, trout and salmon fishing. Tackle for rent, licenses available. Hiking, swimming, hunting. World famous for hospitality. Rooms from $3.00. Complete meals, featuring charcoal broiled steaks. Cocktails and liquors the very best. Open all year.

After owning the lodge for 18 years, the Griers sold to Gregory Zoghby and Ellen Schaub, husband and wife, in 2005. The lodge has a special use permit from Six Rivers National Forest and the ground is owned by them.

Irl Rickabaugh   *DINING ROOM - PATRICK CREEK LODGE*   *After 1946*

ON REDWOOD HIGHWAY BETWEEN
GRANTS PASS & CRESCENT CITY -
Late 1920s.

Jarl deBoer

SMITH RIVER
BETWEEN GRANTS
PASS AND
CRESCENT CITY -
1930s.
Anyone who has ever
traveled Hwy. 199
recognizes this section
of the road.

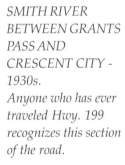

Jarl deBoer

USDA Forest Service   *MOUTH OF JONES CREEK*   *Circa Late 1920s*

GAS RATIONING

During World War II travel on the nation's highways slowed down considerably. It was in 1942 that the rationing of gasoline and other resources began in California. To continue to supply the war effort, gasoline and oil was strictly rationed nationally. Special booklets were issued to allow people to buy limited supplies of gasoline. Emergency services, such as police, fire and ambulance were not restricted. However, the average citizen only received enough fuel to go back and forth to work. Tires were also in short supply as the rubber to manufacture them was needed elsewhere. Motorists were asked to keep their speed below 40 miles per hour by a direct appeal from the President. Later a universal speed limit of 35 miles per hour was enacted. All of this had a negative impact on the tourism business and the mom and pop businesses struggled to survive.

When the war ended in 1945, gas rationing came to a halt and people couldn't wait to get back on the road again. Recreational travel was on the rise with motels doubling in numbers over the next few years.

IDLEWILD AUTO CAMP

Mike Knips   *IDLEWILD AUTO CAMP*   *Early 1930s*
Sign over service station advertises: cabins, cold drinks, meals.

Joe Leger   *IDLEWILD AUTO CAMP*   *Mid-1930s*
Sign out front says: Wirt Lane   Idlewild Auto Camp   Coffee Shop

May 1931–*Sears Roebuck & Co.*
Idlewild Auto Camp
16 cottages, $1.00 to $3.00. Showers.
Camping 50 cents. Open all year.

Jarl deBoer   IDLEWILD RESORT

1952 - *Redwood Empire Assoc.*
Idlewild Auto Camp
32 miles from Crescent City on Highway 199; out of the fog, new deluxe cottages with steam heat, or cabins with cooking facilities. Fisherman's headquarters. Hunting and swimming. Dining room in connection featuring fresh-caught trout dinners. Soft drinks, ice cream, also beer. Chevron gas and oil. Elmer and Pearl Johnston, prop.

Today, Caltrans has their maintenance yard at this site. There has been a state highway maintenance yard in this area since at least the 1930s.

*The original Redwood Highway took a narrow winding route over Oregon Mountain (Hazelview Summit). In order to follow this earlier route make a left turn on **Oregon Mountain Road** at mile 31.31. Be prepared to get a real taste of what these earlier roads were all about. Luckily this road is pretty much deserted today, thank goodness, because it isn't hard to imagine what it must have been like when a logging truck was coming the other way. This route is 7 ¼ miles long and brings you back to Hwy. 199. While driving this route, you have passed over the top of the tunnel and will come out on the other side of the highway. (At around mile 4.75-5.00 you can catch a glimpse of the top of the tunnel entrance.) You need to make a right turn when you return to Hwy. 199 heading east to Grants Pass, Oregon.*

A warning here…I have only taken this road in the summer and early fall and was lucky if I saw any cars on it. So, it is pretty isolated and there are a few rough spots, but nothing serious. However, I would definitely think twice about driving it once the rainy (snow) weather sets in as it is not well maintained.

OREGON MOUNTAIN – HAZEL VIEW SUMMIT

31.31 Oregon Mt.
Road & Hwy. 199

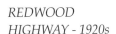
REDWOOD HIGHWAY - 1920s

Jarl deBoer

OREGON MOUNTAIN TUNNEL PROJECT

"On July 8, 1960, a celebration will commemorate the turning of the first shovelful of dirt on the Oregon Mountain tunnel project. The people of Del Norte, California's northwestern county, will rejoice with their neighbors, for the tunnel will remove the last substantial barrier to easy and comfortable access to this land of steep bluffs, deep canyons, and towering mountains. Neighbors to the south will be on hand to cheer another great improvement on the Redwood Highway.

Strong men have been fighting rough terrain in their efforts to travel to and from Del Norte County since 1828. In that year Jedediah Smith, leader of a band of trappers--the first white men to enter this area--came into what is now the county from the southeast. Smith was followed by gold seekers of the 1850s, and a survey for the first road into Crescent City was completed in October, 1854. Called the 'Crescent City and Yreka Plank and Turnpike Road,' its capital stock consisted of 850 shares at $100 per share. The difficulties which confronted the shareholders proved great, and the company was not successful.

In 1855, Ben Kelsey secured subscriptions and labor from the citizens of Crescent City to build a trail from their town to Yreka via the rough Siskiyou Mountains, thence along the banks of the

Siskyou Mountains as seen from near summit of Switchback Grade, On Redwood Highway.
1048-ORFRAY

Jarl deBoer

Klamath and Scott rivers. One of the workers noted that 'the men were a little rough but good workers,' as indeed they must have been. By the end of July they had built a trail through steep sided mountains to Happy Camp on the Klamath River. Portions of this trail, worn deep by the feet of seekers after gold, their pack animals, and by the pack strings supplying the shelves of stores in the diggings, may still be seen in the back country of Del Norte. Possibly the men to the east proved neither as rough nor as good workers as the hardy Del Norters, for the trail never did reach Yreka.

Building adequate roads continued to pose problems for the inhabitants of this county, where one may stand on the damp sands of the seashore and see, but a few miles away, mountains more than five thousand feet high. Major Ward Bradford, who had established a large farm in the valley and coastal plain near the mouth of the Smith River, found the way to market for his products a rough one, both physically and financially. 'Our county,' he wrote, 'was mountainous and of the rockiest character, and there was only one road from the valley to the interior. This road cost $1,000 a mile. This placed a heavy tax on the people.'

Regardless of expense and toil, Del Norters continued their efforts to improve communication with other areas, realizing even then that a successful future for them depended on good roads. Horace Gasquet, a transplanted Frenchman, had a ranch, vineyard and store on a flat in the canyon of Upper Smith River. He employed a large number of Chinese contract laborers, and with their efforts, supervised by an Irish foreman, completed a 23 mile toll road into Oregon in 1886. This road followed the higher ridges, and heavy snowdrifts posed a problem in winter. Often the mail had to be carried by men on skis.

All these roads were built to the northeast, into southern Oregon. A road in any other direction was considered impossible. Ben Kelsey's construction to the east had been restricted to a trail. After the gold rush had subsided, the giant redwoods and Douglas firs nurtured a thriving industry. Logs and lumber were shipped, when weather conditions made it possible, from the exposed harbor of Crescent City, and from deep channels between offshore rocks, where the cargo was loaded by highlines.

Now the hardy natives were ready to tackle the steep hills along the coast to the south. These were not so rocky as the mountains of the interior, their rapidly rising slopes were largely made of clay with often a soft blue mud in the nearly level places. Near the turn of the century, small individual contracts were let, and a road paved with puncheons, four inches thick, was built. The puncheons

at the top of the Switchback Grade
Highest point on Redwood Highway
1035-DBB-MP

Jarl deBoer

were split from straight grained redwoods growing abundantly along the route which climbed up and down Ragged Mountain. A few miles below Crescent City the road came down to the ocean beach. Puncheons were not necessary on the tidal sands, and the last portion of the journey was a dash along the firm sand at low tide.

As it became possible for almost every family to own an automobile, a few tourists ventured into Del Norte County. Their tales of magnificent groves of redwoods, hillsides abloom with azaleas, dogwood and rhododendrons, battles with trout, steelhead and salmon in the mighty Klamath and the unbelievably clear Smith River, influenced their friends to visit this little-known area. At the same time that the trickle of tourists became a sizeable stream, improvements in road building equipment made it possible to construct better highways for their convenience. The power shovel and dump trucks, replacing the hand shovel and the one-or-two horse scraper—known as a fresno—made it practical to build a road composed of gentle grades along the face of the bluffs south of Crescent City. It was no longer necessary to bump, bump, bump over corduroyed puncheons on the steep grades of Ragged Mountain. This new road later proved inadequate. Slides of shattered rock threatening above and ocean waves chewing at the base of the bluffs made widening and improving the alignment impractical. Now a modern well-paved road through groves of great redwoods decorated by pink rhododendrons and freckled tiger lilies gives no hint of earlier difficulties as it runs along the top of Ragged Mountain.

More than 30 years ago (*1920s*), power shovels bit and chewed their way through the hard rock cliffs of Smith River canyon and replaced the old high level Gasquet Road with a new low level road. Grades were easy, and the road, subject only to an occasional light snowfall was easily and quickly removed. Except—no road building job has been easy in Del Norte—where the Oregon Mountain ridge runs squarely across the route. With no way around it, the engineers were forced to design a series of switchbacks up one side and down the other. Snow fell heavily on the high portion, and often froze hard. Plowing snow was difficult on the sharp curves, and was usually complicated by stalled cars which had skidded to the low side of the banked turns.

A tunnel was the only solution—a dream once considered impossible to translate into reality. Meantime, a huge lumber industry had grown up, myriads of tourists were enjoying pleasant and interesting vacations, commercial fishing and ocean shipping had become sizeable industries, and large bodies of low grade ore had been discovered. The people of the rich valleys of southeastern

Touring The Old Redwood Highway

Oregon and of part of Nevada were seeking a short route to the sea.

So the Del Norters, modern counterparts of the earlier Ben Kelseys and Horace Gasquets, still 'a little rough, but good workers,' steadily laboring, on July 8 (*1960*), will see their latest efforts begin to show results. At last, all roads to Del Norte County will be wide open."[24]

COLLIER TUNNEL

33.51 Hwy. 199

"The Randolph Collier Tunnel (1,835 feet long) and approaches, located two miles south of the California-Oregon border on U.S. 199, was dedicated and opened to traffic on July 20, 1963, after nearly 3 ½ years of construction. The completed project has a total length of 4.3 miles of modern two-lane highway. It replaces more than seven miles of narrow, twisting mountain road which formerly snaked its way over the Hazelview Summit of Oregon Mountain. On the road over the summit a motorist was required to negotiate five steep switchbacks and make a total of 144 turns, many of which were posted for speeds of 25-mph and less. As a contrast the new road has been designed for 60-mph speeds, and has but 16 curves."[25] A complete relocation of US 199 in the area will eliminate difficult snow removal, the continuously steep grade, improve alignment and reduce distance over the old road. The miles of long twisting roads that made transportation so hazardous between the interior and the coast will be eliminated.

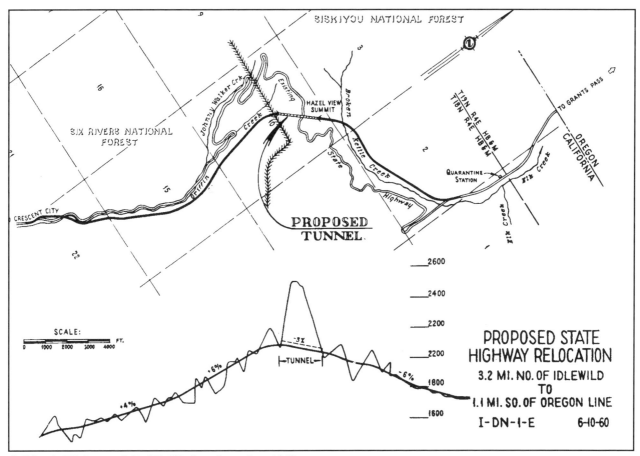

California Highways & Public Works - Sept.-Oct. 1960
Courtesy of California Department of Transportation Library

[24] *"Oregon Mountain Tunnel Project," by Hugh Ross.*

[25] *California Highways & Public Works - Sept.-Oct. 1963. Courtesy of California Department of Transportation Library.*

SISKIYOU MOUNTAIN CAMP

Siskiyou Mountain Camp

43 miles north of Crescent City on the Redwood Highway.

SISKIYOU MOUNTAIN COFFEE SHOP

Mr. and Mrs. W. F. Hayter, proprietors. Meals at all hours.

HAPPY JACK'S GARAGE

The guy who makes motoring a pleasure.

The Humboldt Times - Sept. 14, 1933

Irl Rickabaugh   *SISKIYOU MOUNTAIN CAMP*   *Circa 1932*

Located across the road from the Inspection Station near the Oregon border.

May 1931 – *Sears Roebuck & Co.*
Siskiyou Mountain Camp
45 miles N.E. of Crescent City, 12 cottages, $1.50. Bedding 50 cents. Showers. Camping 50 cents.

Early 1940's – *Redwood Empire Assoc.*
Siskiyou Mountain Camp
Forrest T. Dunham, Proprietor
Located 43 miles northeast of Crescent City on Highway 199. 1/2 mile south of Oregon state line. Elevation 1700. Cool, shady camp on small lake, fishing, swimming. Single cabins $1.00 to $1.50, hotel style. Double cabins $2.50 to $3.50, hotel style. Excellent meals at coffee shop. No mosquitoes. Open all year.

Jarl deBoer   *INSPECTION STATION*   *Early 1930s*

36.41 Hwy. 199

Arlene Hartin   *OREGON STATE LINE*

We have made it to the Oregon border. This book ends here at the state line, but the Redwood Highway actually continues on to Grants Pass, Oregon. We have traveled through the redwoods, up and down mountains, across rivers, along the ocean, across valleys, and through towns. Del Norte County is not a very big county but it certainly has its share of scenery and varied terrain. Today, Highway 101 from the Humboldt/Del Norte county line to the Oregon border is 46.10 miles. The distance on Highway 199 to the Oregon border is 36.41 miles. It certainly seems a lot bigger.

This is the 3rd and last book on the old Redwood Highway. Along the way, we have traveled through Mendocino, Humboldt and Del Norte counties. I have spent seven years working on this road. Even now it is hard to realize how many auto camps, auto courts, early motels, service stations and novelty shops once lined the road. So much was here and now it is almost all gone.

Hopefully, this book has given you a whole new perspective of the old road. Remember to keep an eye out for that old auto camp or a piece of the old highway. I hope that you enjoyed the journey. Drive safe!

NORTH TO OREGON
FT. DICK --
TOWN OF SMITH RIVER

Redwood Highway Review - Dec. 1928

Courtesy Metsker Maps/Janssen Inc.
Shading on Hwy. 101 added.

DEL NORTE COUNTY - 1949

Now that we have traveled the Redwood Highway (Highway 199) to the Oregon border, it is time to take a little side trip. Going back to Crescent City, let's take a ride north to the Oregon border. This road takes you to Fort Dick, the town of Smith River and north to Brookings, Oregon. This section of highway has had several names and numbers over the years. It has been known as Highway 1, the Roosevelt Highway, Highway 71 and Highway 101. I've also seen it called the Coast Highway Del Norte Coast Highway, and the Oregon Coast Highway.

On the northern end of Crescent City make a left turn on **Northcrest Drive.** You will follow this road until it turns into **Lake Earl Drive** which will take you through the town of **Fort Dick** (around 8 miles). Continue north for about a mile and stay to the right. This will bring you back to today's **Hwy. 101**. Remember things looked a lot different before the highway was realigned through here in 1954.

Make a left turn on **Hwy. 101** and cross over the **Smith River Bridge** (Dr. Ernest M. Fine Memorial Bridge). Then it's a left hand turn on **Fred Haight Drive.** Continue on this road until **First Street** (flashing traffic signal at the intersection) where you will make another left. This is the **Town of Smith River** and was once a busy place when the highway came through here. Continue on First Street until you come to the curve and stay to the right on **Sarina Road.** Once again, you are back to today's **Highway 101**.

Northcrest Drive
Crescent City

AZALEA LODGE

1950 – *National Auto Club*
Azalea Lodge
Built 1936.
6 modern units.
$4.00 up.

Irl Rickabaugh   *AZALEA LODGE*

Building New Cabins – *June 23 (probably early 1940s)*
"Percy Jordan and son Philip are making good headway on the improvement of Azalea Lodge a mile north of this city on the Oregon Coast Highway. Three new cabins are being built, the former buildings are being remodeled and the grounds are to be landscaped.
A new water system has also been installed and the place modernized in general. When complete Azalea Lodge will be one of the best auto courts in the city."

Del Norte Triplicate

JEFFORD'S COURT

Early 1940's – *Redwood Empire Assoc.*
Jefford's Court
1 ¼ miles north of Crescent City on 101 Highway. Cabins, new modern and comfortable. 1, 2, 3, and 4 rooms, all private showers, toilet and garage. Beds equipped with new coil springs and innerspring mattresses, gas or electric cooking facilities. Rates: $1.00 to $4.00. Coffee shop and Shell service in connection with court. Near good fishing and seacoast. Open all year.

FIREPLACE COURT

Mr. & Mrs. George Baguley were operating Fireplace Court in 1946.

It is possible that Fireplace Court may have been called Jefford's Court earlier.

Del Norte County Historical Society   FIREPLACE COURT   *1940s*

Calling Paul Bunyan:
Clearing Del Norte Freeway is Job for Legendary Logger

"Many times during the past six months the McCammon-Wunderlich Company has wished that the legendary Paul Bunyan and his great Blue Ox, Babe, could be put on the payroll to help with the monumental task of clearing 72 acres of right of way, much of it through dense virgin and second-growth redwood forest. This king-sized logging job was part of the contract awarded in April of this year for clearing and grading a 5 ½ mile portion of US 101 between US 199 and the Smith River Bridge in Del Norte County. Also included in the contract was approximately one-half mile of construction along US 199 at the south end of the project. The completion of this contract early this fall will result in a graded roadbed on two-lane, limited access freeway standards of the 5 ½ mile portion of US 101. The base and surfacing are to be placed next year under separate contract. When completed, this portion will by-pass a 9 ½ mile section of US 101 which is narrow and winding with undulating grade and encroaching trees and stumps, which makes hazardous driving conditions for the traveling public."

California Highway & Public Works - Sept.-Oct. 1954
Courtesy of California Department of Transportation Library

Note: This realignment eliminated the Northcrest/Lake Earl Drive section of the highway.

PATTERSON'S CAMP

1930 – *Western Guide*
Patterson's Camp
7 miles north (Crescent City)
Roosevelt Highway. 12 cottages,
$1.50-$3.50. Bath, toilet, kitchenette, laundry, modern cabins,
sleeping cabins, fuel, lights, water,
bedding furnished. Shade, playground, stream or lake swimming,
beach, pool, fishing, hunting,
guides. Garage, service station,
grocery, meat market, fresh milk,
watchman.

REDWOOD PARADISE

Redwood Paradise Auto Court 7 miles north of Crescent City on Coast highway. New and modern cabins equipped with Flamo Gas and other conveniences. Play ground, swings and sand pit for the children. Out door fire place. Enjoy your vacation in the sunshine. Service station and store. Fishing in Smith River and Lake Earl.

The Humboldt Times - Sept. 14, 1933

This auto court may have become Skeleton Park.

Official Highway Guide for Del Norte County - 1941

OREGON COAST HIGHWAY - NORTH
CRESCENT CITY TO OREGON LINE - U.S. 101

.0 **SHELL SERVICE STATION No. 689**
   Myron W. Stevens, Mgr.
   9th & L Sts.
.1 County Hospital and Fair Grounds
.2 Junction U.S.199, east
.2 Highway maintenance yard
1.5 BLUE RIBBON BAKERY; Wakefield Store. "Real Home Made Bread."
   M.G. Stevens, prop.
1.9 Pine Grove Store
3.4 **CRESCENT CITY NURSERY. Cut flowers, bulbs and shrubbery.**
   Raymond K. Marks, prop.
3.7 Alder Road, turn right
3.8 Malone Ave., turn right
4.5 Never Dying Redwood, turn right
8.7 TOWN OF FORT DICK
   FORT DICK GENERAL STORE
   E. Stephen, prop.
10.0 The Dr. Ernest M. Fine Memorial Bridge, crossing Smith River.
   Good swimming.
10.1 North Bank Road, turn right to U.S. 199 east.
12.2 Rowdy Creek School
13.8 TOWN OF SMITH RIVER
   DEL NORTE MILK PRODUCTS CO. Smith River phone 121
15.2 **VALLEY VIEW AUTO COURT**
20.1 **WHITE ROCK AUTO PARK; gas station. Near the Oregon Line.**
20.5 California quarantine station
20.9 Oregon state line

REDWOOD SKELETON PARK – SKELETON PARK

1949 – *Redwood Empire Assoc.* Redwood Skeleton Park Picturesque tree oddities. Seven miles north of Crescent City. Highway 101. See the 'Picture Frame Stump,' illustrated in "Ripley's Believe It or Not." Cabin accommodations, trailer space, camping. Near the ocean. Excellent fishing in nearby Smith River, Crescent City, California.

Irl Rickabaugh   SKELETON PARK

Skeleton Park was a tourist attraction with its great redwood stumps sending forth grotesque and twisted branches or earnest sprouts of new growth. Located just south of MALARKEY FOREST, thru which the narrow highway meandered around giant redwoods. Huge logging trucks were slowed down to skirt the redwood trunks, sometimes forcing oncoming traffic to halt. Many a naive or unalert driver had an accident, sometimes fatal.

1952

I was unable to find the exact location of Skeleton Park. However, I believe it was in the area of Chicama or Maeghan Way, just south of Pelican Bay State Prison.

Irl Rickabaugh   SKELETON PARK

Gary Ingle   *TOWN OF FORT DICK*   1929

The building on the left is selling Shell gasoline and kerosene.
FISK sign hanging advertises Tires Tubes Service Station.
White building across from car - Fort Dick Garage with gas pump.

As Highway 101 approached the town of Fort Dick, it traversed through some of the finest stands of trees in the northern Redwood Empire. There were still plenty of vehicles hurrying along but the road seemed quieter now that you were off the heavily traveled route from San Francisco to Crescent City.

Located in town was the Fort Dick General Store (Market) built in the early logging and mill days. It was known as the Hobbs-Wall Lumber Company at that time. John Johnson purchased the store during World War I and ran it for over 20 years. In 1949 Lloyd and Helen Waterman owned the business. The store was a large old wooden building and its floor was worn by the feet of patrons searching its depths for groceries, hardware, garden tools, housewares, sunscreen, fishing tackle and special treats such as ice cream bars and popsicles. Alongside the front of the store were the old gas pumps.

Until 1955, Hwy. 101 still ambled through Fort Dick and this little community surrounded by farmlands was a busy and thriving place. The old mercantile eventually burned down.

SMITH RIVER BRIDGE

California Highways & Public Works - April 1941
Courtesy of California Department of Transportation Library

OLD COUNTY BRIDGE   *Built 1907*
This bridge became part of the Redwood Highway.

Due to a continuing increase in traffic over this section of the highway, 9½ miles north of Crescent City, a new steel and concrete girder bridge across the Smith River was opened in 1941. This bridge was placed on a new alignment down stream from the old and narrow steel truss and timber trestle bridge built in 1907 by Del Norte County. Although adequate for the traffic of its day, the old bridge was too narrow for modern traffic needs and beyond repairing.

The new bridge was dedicated to Dr. Ernest M. Fine on May 30, 1949.

This bridge opened a new and direct route between Crescent City and Smith River in the horse and buggy days.

Just north of the bridge is the junction of Hwy. 101 and North Bank Road (Hwy. 197). In earlier days this was known as Hwy. 81. This route takes you to Hwy. 199.

Jarl deBoer   *CLOSE UP VIEW OF THE OLD BRIDGE*

TOWN OF SMITH RIVER

1929

Gary Ingle

SMITH RIVER
The Redwood Highway went to the left on First Street.

1929 - Buildings L-R
Far left - water tank on roof - Valley Market
Sign on building for C.H. Alton's Circus
On corner - Smith River Bank
Building with truck in front advertises
  rooms and pool
Next door - Store for Men
Next building - Ice Cream
2nd truck - large white sign overhanging
  Smith River Inn

Circa 1940
On left corner - Coffee Shop - Fountain Service
On right, 1st car - Smith River Post Office
Hight's General Store
  Notice the gas pumps in front of the store

Circa 1940

SMITH RIVER

Joe Leger

No. 11-B Revised to June 16, 1934

OREGON COAST
and
REDWOOD HIGHWAY

PORTLAND
AND
ASTORIA
TO
SAN FRANCISCO

AMERICA'S
MOST
SCENIC
ROUTE

OREGON MOTOR STAGES
2521 S. W. HOOD AVENUE   PORTLAND, OREGON
YAMHILL STAGE DEPOT   PHONE ATWATER 5171

SAN FRANCISCO   75 FIFTH STREET   PHONE DOUGLAS 4664
PACIFIC GREYHOUND TERMINAL

Courtesy of Bruce Brunell

Stage Stops were:
Gold Beach (Central S.S.)
Pistol River
Carpenterville
Brookings (Stage Depot)
State Line
Smith River
Crescent City (Pharrs' Fountain)
Crescent City (Lunch)
Big Tree Park
Requa Junction
Klamath (P.O. Stage Depot)
Orick
Stone Lagoon
Big Lagoon Bridge
Trinidad (Model Garage)
Moonstone
Crannell Junction
Clam Beach
McKinleyville
Weaverville Junction
Arcata (S.D.) 8th & H
Eureka (S.D.) 4th & E
Fernbridge
Scotia
Weott
Garberville
Lanes Redwood Flat
Willits
Ukiah
Santa Rosa
San Francisco (75 5th)

At one time, the original highway (**Sarina Road**) continued straight across Hwy. 101 and continued up the hill on **Ocean View Drive**. This is a really pretty drive and at 4.6 miles you will come across a really nice example of an old concrete highway bridge. Following the road all the way it will bring you back to **Hwy. 101** a short distance south of the state line. On the Oregon side of the border there is still a section of road called Ocean View Drive... so it must have continued across the state line at one time. This section of highway was used until the mid-to-late 1930's.

After **Ocean View Drive** was no longer used, you would have come out on **Sarina Road** and made a left hand turn on **Hwy. 101**. This section of highway has followed the same route since that time. But remember, the roads would have been a lot narrower and probably lacking the shoulders we enjoy today. Follow **Hwy. 101** to the Oregon border.

VALLEY VIEW MOTOR COURT

40.18 - SW Corner
Sarina Rd. & Hwy. 101

■■■■■■■■■■■■■■■■■■■■■■■■
VALLEY VIEW MOTOR COURT
New and Modern
For the Best in Rest
Close by the Giant Redwoods
Vance Bolick—Fred McFarland
■■■■■■■■■■■■■■■■■■■■■■■■

National Road Service - 1941

1950 – *National Auto Club*
Valley View Auto Court
Built 1938. 6 modern units. $4.50.

DEL NORTE AUTO PARK

Ocean View Dr.

As far as I can tell, Del Norte Auto Park was located on the southern end of Ocean View Drive. It appears there may have also been another auto camp in this area.

Irl Rickabaugh   DEL NORTE AUTO PARK   Late 1920s
Sign on top of the building: Del Norte Trout Farm.

1934 – *Shell Directory*
Del Norte Auto Park
16 miles north Crescent City. Community toilets and showers, kitchen with dishes. Grocery and restaurant nearby. Open garages. 75 cents-$1.00. Extra charge for bedding and linen.

CASTLE ROCK CAMP – SHIP ASHORE

This resort is located on the Smith River at the end of Chinook Street.

Irl Rickabaugh   CASTLE ROCK AUTO CAMP   1936

In 1941, Joe and Betty Sierka purchased the Castle Rock Camp situated on 368 acres on the Smith River. The business consisted of 12 small cabins, a dilapidated cannery, a lunch counter and a boat rental. Since the area was renowned for its fishing, the Sierkas opened a fine tackle shop and enticed fishermen to their resort. Their business flourished until the late 1940s when the lodge building housing the dining room, tackle shop, motel office and living quarters burned to the ground. It was then that Joe came up with the idea of purchasing an ocean-sized ship to replace the lodge. Purchased in Oakland the ship definitely had seen better days. It was rusty, had numerous coats of peeling paint over the beautiful teak and mahogany interior, no motor and was waiting to be cut into scrap. The ship was towed from Oakland to Eureka and on the second attempt arrived successfully at the Castle Rock Resort on the Smith River. The remodeled ship was opened on July 4, 1950 to much festivity and a crowd of hundreds. Over the years, the boat would house a restaurant, private museum, tackle shop, gifts and the family's living quarters. Later, a new restaurant was built not too far from the ship.

The Westbrook family purchased the resort in 1964 and moved the ship inland next to Highway 101 where it still sits today. A new 32-unit motel was completed in 1965 and still sits along the riverbank where the ship once stood.

Irl Rickabaugh   Late 1940s

Irl Rickabaugh

Crescent City H.S. Yearbook - 1945

Building housed the dining room, tackle shop, office and living quarters. Burned down in the late 1940s.

Irl Rickabaugh   CASTLE ROCK LODGE   *Late 1940s*

Arlene Hartin   *S. S. CASTLE ROCK*   *Early 1950s*
The boat was located right next to the Smith River for many years and later moved near Hwy. 101.

Yacht Placed Successfully In Smith River

SMITH RIVER, Calif.—"On a second attempt to run the narrow treacherous channel at the mouth of the Smith River, the 156 foot German built yacht Caritas was successfully towed to a safe anchorage by the tug Prospector, skippered by Capt. Oscar Huffman of the Coggeshall Launch Company of Eureka.

Several hundred people from Del Norte county and southern Oregon lined the banks of the narrow river at high tide about noon today to watch the tricky maneuver, which ended in failure last August because of a heavy ground swell which developed at the critical time when the tide was just right. The ship was towed back to Eureka and laid up until February 16, when she was towed into Crescent City harbor and arrangements were made to make the second try which was successful today.

The *Caritas* was built by the Krupp Company at Kiel, Germany, in 1925 for A.L. Bartram of New York. During World War II she was operated by the navy as a patrol boat and was known as the *SS Garnett*. She was purchased last July by M.J. Sierka, proprietor of Castle Rock Camp resort, rechristened the *S.S. Castle Rock*, and will be permanently anchored inside the mouth of the river and operated as a resort lodge to replace the original lodge building which was completely destroyed by fire in the fall of 1948.

The *Castle Rock* is more than twice as large as any ship which ever entered the Smith River, and is the first ship to enter the mouth since 1925, when the *Martha II* of Eureka, a general cargo vessel 75 feet long and about 30 tons gross weight, made its final voyage under the command of Capt. Ole Olsen.

The Martha II handled general commodities consigned to Del Norte county farmers and merchants and carried back canned salmon, redwood products and chrome ore. Since 1925 there has been no commercial shipping of any sort from the mouth of the Smith River."

Del Norte Triplicate - Feb. 17, 1950

Jarl deBoer

1954 – *Redwood Empire Assoc.*
S.S. Castle Rock—Ship On Shore
Located at the mouth of the Smith River. Trout, Salmon and Steelhead fishing; crabs, clams, surf fishing; duck hunting, boats, motors, guides. Cottages, trailer park and camping grounds. Cocktail Lounge and Dining Room aboard the ship anchored at the dock. Grocery store. Moderate rates. Open all year. For reservation phone Smith River 346 or write M.J. Sierka, Smith River.

SALMON HARBOR RESORT

Salmon Harbor Rd.
& Hwy. 199

Irl Rickabaugh   *Circa 1956*

RIVER'S END AUTO COURT

Irl Rickabaugh　　　　RIVER'S END AUTO COURT　　　　*Built in 1939*

Early 1940s – Redwood Empire Assoc. River's End Auto Court Located 4 miles north of Smith River on Highway 101. A new court beautifully situated on the ocean offering modern accommodations at reasonable rates. Plenty of space for trailers. An attractive coffee shop in connection, serving delicious meals. Open all year.

DEL NORTE "THE LAST OF THE WEST"

"There is practically fifteen billion feet of timber in Del Norte County, only a very small area having been cut. The Redwood Groves are more beautiful than any others, as the dense under-growth give them an appearance of some tropical jungle. Oh! A wonderful jungle because there is nothing to fear. There is great electrical energy going to waste that some day will be harnessed and made to pay toll.

Being isolated from the busy whirl of commerce, having no rail communication, and in the past, roads that were nearly impassable, it has retained all the natural beauty and wildness of the 'Old West.' It is a fact that old traditions so cling to 'Del Norte' that people still believe the roads impassable. It hardly seems reasonable to think that a stage line would send three large stages a day over a road that is in anything but very good condition. Being a new road, there is some construction on the highway at all times but things are so well managed that very little inconvenience is felt by anyone. Do not let anyone turn you back, now is the time to see this wonder land, before the hand of man sweeps away the beauties of nature.

No better fishing or hunting exists anywhere. Bear, cougar, coon, mink, marten, skunk and civet cat; deer and elk, grouse, quail and duck; salmon, trout, eel, flounder crabs, clams and surf fish, are among the most prevalent. Mountain streams, two large rivers and many miles of ocean front make Del Norte an ideal vacation land. With Pebble Beach, the million-dollar breakwater, the beautiful Lake Earl, five miles of smooth hard sand, and many other things too numerous to mention. There are many beautiful camp sites and modern hotels."

Redwood Highway Review – Aug. 15, 1927

WHITE ROCK AUTO PARK – WHITE ROCK COTTAGES

There was a service station advertised in the early 1940s.

Jarl deBoer   WHITE ROCK COTTAGES   *Late 1930s*

1937 – *California State Automobile Assoc.*
White Rock Auto Park
1/4 mile south of Oregon line on U.S. 101. No phone. 10 cottages. Private showers and toilets. Housekeeping facilities, dishes and cooking utensils included. Extra charge for bedding. Hot running water. Electric lights and gas stoves. Locked garages. Coffee shop on premises. $2.50-$5.00. 50 trailers, electric connections, community laundry, central sanitary conveniences.

1949 – *Redwood Empire Assoc.*
White Rock Cottages
At Oregon line. Coast Highway 101. Finest fishing and hunting. By the sea. Beautiful sand beach, surf bathing, spring water. Dining room and cocktail lounge on grounds. Phone 16-T-13, Smith River. Mr. and Mrs. H.A. (Sandy) Sanders.

Irl Rickabaugh   WHITE ROCK COTTAGES   *Late 1940s*

TYLER'S STATE LINE MOTEL – STATE LINE MOTEL

Irl Rickabaugh   *TYLER'S STATE LINE MOTEL*   *Late 1940s*

1952 - *Redwood Empire Assoc.*
State Line Motel
At the California and Oregon line, Coast Highway 101. Cabins with kitchenettes and all electric heat. Service station. Surf casting, salmon and trout fishing. Vacation spot, summer and fall. Coffee shop with home cooking. Moderate rates. Beautiful marine view of Pelican Bay. Open all year 'round. B. L. Tyler, owner.

Sign on front advertises:
Wild Berry Pie
Chicken Pie
Sea Foods
Sandwiches
Cigars
Candies
Soft Drinks

Joe Leger   *TYLER'S STATE LINE MOTEL -- COFFEE SHOP*   *Late 1940s*

1950 -*National Auto Club* State Line Motel Built 1946. 12 modern units. $3.50

Sign out front: Last chance to save 2 cents a gallon on gas.

Irl Rickabaugh   TYLER'S STATE LINE MOTEL
Notice the Inspection Station in the background.

INSPECTION STATION

46.10 Hwy. 101

"The bug stops here! That's the purpose of the Smith River Inspection Station at the California-Oregon state line, commonly and affectionately known as the 'Bug Station'. The question you'll hear them ask most of the time is 'do you have any fruit?'

The station has been in its present location since the 1930's, before that, it was located at South Beach in Crescent City for a short time. The building itself has remained the same structurally except for a few modifications along the way—like raising the height of the pass-through areas to accommodate the larger vehicles that came along as the auto industry progressed.

The area around the station has changed, though. There used to be a clear view of the ocean as far as the eye could see to the north, but houses and businesses now cover most of that space. In fact, when the station was in its early days, it served as a guard lookout for possible Japanese invasions during World War II."

Irl Rickabaugh   INSPECTION STATION   1947
The station was used to check for possible crop pests coming across the border from Oregon and points north. Shown from the south side in this photo.

Well, this is the end of the road. I hope that you enjoyed your trip and I'll catch you on the highway.
Diane Hawk

Triplicate - May 29, 2002

SOURCES

A History of the Six Rivers National Forest...Commemorating the First 50 Years, U.S. Dept. of Agriculture, Forest Service, Pacific Southwest Region, Pamela A. Conners, Oct. 1997.

"And High Water," Pictorial Review of Northwestern California's Disastrous Christmas Flood 1955, compiled and published by publishers of The Pacific Logger, Eureka, CA.

Bancroft Library, U.C. Berkeley, Berkeley, CA.

California Dept. of Transportation (Caltrans), District 1 Office, 1656 Union, Eureka, CA.

California Dept. of Transportation Library and History Center, 1120 N St., Room 1430, Sacramento, CA.

California Highways, 1924-Oct. 1927 (California Dept. of Transportation).

California Highways & Public Works, Nov. 1927-1970 (California Dept. of Transportation).

California HISTORIAN (California Historical Society magazine). www.californiahistorian.com

Clarke Historical Museum, 3rd & E Street, Eureka, CA.

California State Automobile Association, San Francisco, CA.

Crescent City Directory.

Crescent City High School Yearbooks.

Dark Disaster, Tsunami; March 28, 1964, Crescent City, CA (Wallace Griffin).

deBoer, Jarl. (Redwood Highway postcard website). www.tunneltree.com/redwood/index.html

Del Norte Business Directory & Guide Book

Del Norte County Historical Society, 577 H Street, Crescent City, CA 95531. www.delnortehistory.org

Del Norte Triplicate (*The Daily Triplicate*) Crescent City, CA.

Humboldt County Historical Society, 703 Eighth Street, Eureka, CA. www.humboldthistory.org

Humboldt County Library, Humboldt Room, 1313 3rd St., Eureka, CA.

Humboldt State University Library, Arcata, CA.

Journal Society for Commercial Archeology, "The Redwood Highway," Vol. 16, No. 2, Fall 1998.

Metsker Maps/Janssen Inc., 7530 28th Street W, Suite A, University Place, WA 98466, 253-588-5222.

Motor Land (California State Automobile Association).

Redwood Empire Association, 1431 Sycamore St., Napa, CA 94559 (415) 292-5527. www.redwoodempire.com

Redwood Highway Review (Redwood Empire Association).

Redwood National Park & State Park History. www.cr.nps.gov

Rohde, Jerry and Gisela. *Redwood National & State Parks –Tales, Trails & Auto Tours*, McKinleyville, Mountain Home Books, 1994.

Rohde, Jerry and Gisela. Best Short Hikes in Redwood National & State Parks, Seattle, WA, 2004.

Sacramento Bee, *"Land of the Giants,"* March 4, 1990.

Six Rivers National Recreation Area, 1330 Bayshore Way, Eureka, CA.

Smith River National Recreation Area, Highway 199, Gasquet, CA.

The Humboldt Historian, (Humboldt County Historical Society). www.humboldthistory.org

The Humboldt Times (*Times Standard*) Eureka, CA.

The Press Democrat, Santa Rosa, CA 95402.

West Coast Telephone Co.

Travel Directory Sources:

American Automobile Association

American Drive Guides

Associated Oil

Automobile Club of Southern California

Beige & White

California State Automobile Assoc.

National Automobile Club

Peck-Judah Travel Bureaus

Redwood Empire Association

Sears & Roebuck Company

Shell Oil Company

Western Travel Guides

INDEX

ORDER FORM

If you are interested in ordering a book please use the enclosed form or information.

Send to:
Hawk Mountaintop Publishing
P.O. Box 88
Piercy, CA 95587

Purchaser _____

Address _____

City _____ State _____ Zip _____

If you would like book shipped to a different address please include information.

No. of Books

_____ *Touring the Old Redwood Highway*
Del Norte County
Diane Hawk
@ $20.95 _____

_____ *Touring the Old Redwood Highway*
Humboldt County
Diane Hawk
@ $23.95 _____

_____ *Touring the Old Redwood Highway*
Mendocino County
Diane Hawk
@ $22.95 _____

_____ *A Glance Back*
Northern Mendocino County History
Margarite Cook & Diane Hawk
@ $22.95 _____

_____ *In the Early Days*
Southern Humboldt History 1853-1920
Margarite Cook & Diane Hawk
@ $20.95 _____

California residents only **.0725 tax** _____

Shipping & Handling _____
$3.50 first book, $1.00 each additional book

Please send check or money order **Total Amount** _____
payable to Hawk Mountaintop Publishing.

Thank you for your order!